# CONTENTS

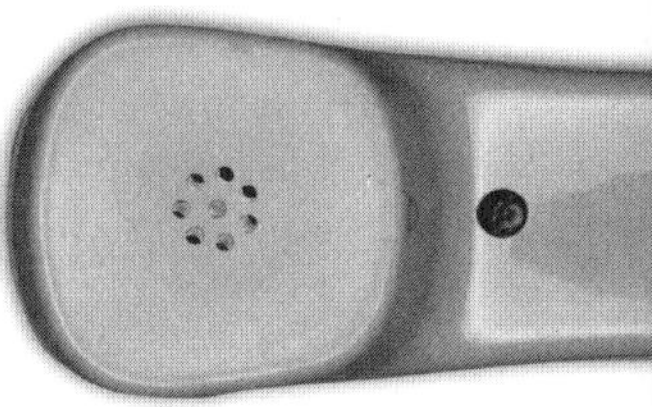

# PART 1

## WELCOME TO MY WORLD

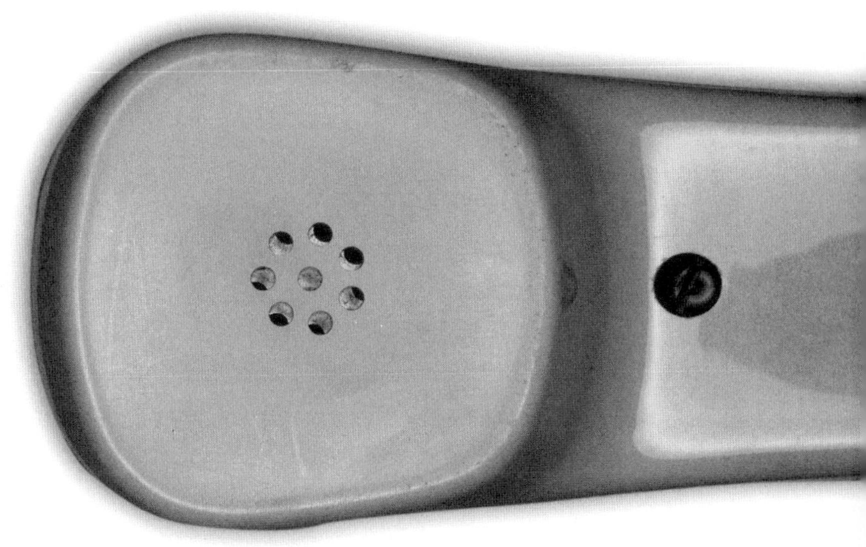

# CHAPTER ONE

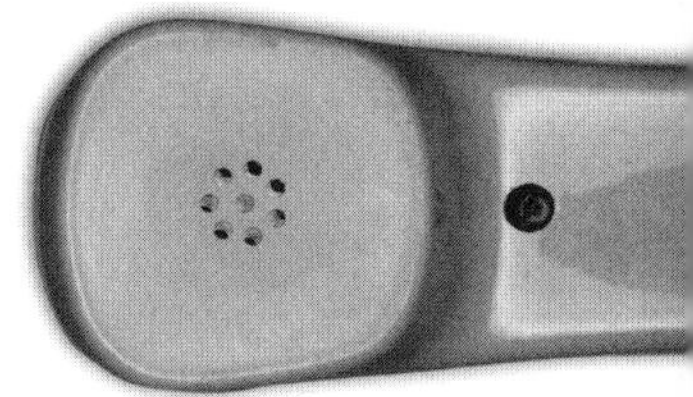

# Selling black cats at midnight

MAKING 100,000 COLD CALLS . . . IT'S BEEN quite an education! Over the last twenty-five years, I've called over 100,000 business decision makers throughout the United States, selling software, hardware, advertising, training, and technical information. I've dialed businesses of all sizes representing virtually every industry, from healthcare to manufacturing, retail to wholesale, financial services to education. I've both purchased call lists and created them. I've used sophisticated call management software and index cards. I've spoken with VIPs of all descriptions and more receptionists than I care to remember. I've generated leads, arranged appointments, and sold products directly.

What I haven't done is call consumers at home. I don't believe in it. Calling folks while they're trying to eat dinner seems rude and unnecessary. Besides, individual consumers have been so abused by fast-talking scam artists that legitimate telemarketers don't have a chance.

I prefer selling business products to businesspeople during normal business hours. The process is surprisingly cordial. In fact, in all my years of business-to-business (B2B) telemarketing, fewer than ten people have ever hung-up on me in anger. Many prospects seem to welcome my calls, glad to learn the latest about this or that without having to research the marketplace themselves.

As a telemarketer, I'm like a blind man selling black cats at midnight. I can't see my customers, and they can't see me or my product. Hour after hour, I repeat my pitch, straining to be heard in the dark above the other hawkers, searching for the perfect words spoken in the perfect way that will lure the curious for a closer look.

When someone finally stops to listen, I have less than thirty seconds to explain who I am, what I'm selling, and why the person should listen for another thirty seconds. I have less than thirty seconds to push an unconscious button within the listener's psyche signaling that I'm safe and worthy of consideration. I have less than thirty seconds to condense a complex conglomeration of technical product features into a simple, commonsense concept that the listener can immediately understand and remember. I have less than thirty seconds to convince the listener that my product will significantly lower costs, increase revenue, or both.

When I'm not talking, I'm listening—listening to every word, sigh, cough, and background noise, instantly analyzing every sound for subtle clues about the speaker's unspoken motives and concerns.

Like a chemical reaction, the conversation unfolds at lightning speed. In a flash, my time is over, and I'm either a hero or a goat. In the time it takes to sip a cup of coffee, I turn into a prince or a pumpkin . . . usually the latter.

Over the years, I've gained an uncommon tolerance for rejection. At least 95,000 of the prospects I've called in my career were not interested in what I was selling. Few people can tolerate so much bad news.

For that reason, I've always had a job. I'm like a gravedigger—somebody has to do it, but nobody wants to. Every company wants someone to make cold calls, but few have employees willing to do the dirty work. Time after time, I've seen experienced sales reps use any excuse to avoid dialing the phone. Typically, they're not interested in wading through hundreds of rejections to find a few diamonds in the rough.

At the end of the day, physically exhausted and emotionally spent, I count my coins and remember the two eternal rules of telemarketing:

1. If you don't sell, you don't eat.
2. If you keep calling, you'll always sell.

# CHAPTER TWO

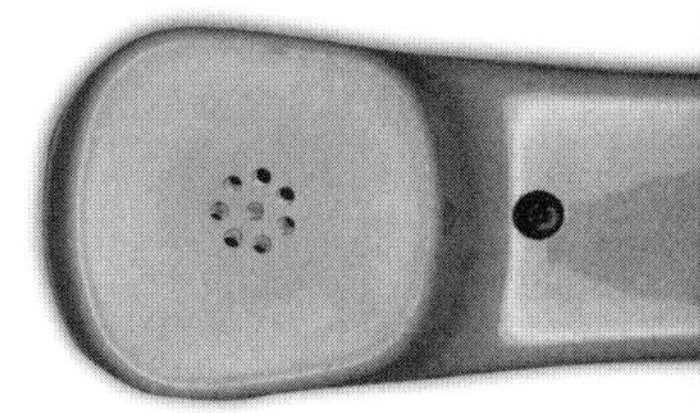

# Nobody does it better

COMPARED TO OTHER SALES STRATEGIES, telemarketing offers significant advantages, including surprise, personal contact, immediate feedback, flexibility, and cost effectiveness.

## ELEMENT OF SURPRISE

### Whisper in their ear.

Telemarketing interjects an element of surprise that person-to-person sales calls do not. When you show up for an appointment, the buyer is expecting you. He has reserved time and energy for you. He is already thinking about you, your company, and your product before you sit down.

A cold call from a telemarketer is totally different. The buyer is not expecting you and hasn't reserved any time for you. He's simply going about his business, putting out fires, trying to please the boss, juggling responsibilities at home, and thinking about where he's going to eat lunch. E-mails are popping up on his screen. His to-do list still isn't getting done. He's deciding which calls to return.

In the middle of this whirlwind, you call—a strange person from a strange company with a strange product looking for money. You're a gnat on the nose of the elephant, a speck in the eye of the tiger. You're uninvited, unexpected, and generally unwelcome.

But thanks to the power of the telephone, you are there in the buyer's ear. Like the guy who yells "fire!" in a crowded theater, you are heard above the cacophony, at least for an instant. Depending on what you say and how you say it, you'll be heralded as a hero or just another bum who gets tossed out in the street.

Once you get the decision maker's attention, you never know what he'll say. You might get exceedingly lucky and be greeted with an enthusiastic "Yes" on the other end of the line, or exceedingly unlucky and get chewed out for calling. You might encounter an objection or just vague puzzlement. You might be asked a question or hear a long silence.

Regardless, you must instantly deliver the right words in the right tone at the right moment. Parry and thrust. You're a fencer facing an unpredictable opponent.

## PERSONAL CONTACT

### Make a connection.

Despite the mass coverage of direct mail, Internet, radio, TV, newspaper, and magazine marketing, none of these establish personal contacts with the buyer. Supposedly in this electronic age, human contact is becoming unnecessary, which would be true if we were all robots. In reality, we are flesh-and-blood, emotional creatures who must have personal contact with other human beings in order to survive.

Sure, millions of purchases are made on the Internet every day without a human salesperson. But what happens when the product breaks? When the customer can't understand how to use it? Then the person who was perfectly happy to buy from a machine wants to talk with a human being. Dell Computer, for example, found that its online sales suffered when its customer service failed to match the quality of its merchandise.

The larger and more complex the product or service, the more essential the need for a human being to sell it. Telemarketing meets that need, establishing a trusting emotional frame of reference with the buyer upon which both initial sales and long-term customer relationships can evolve.

## IMMEDIATE FEEDBACK

### Test the water.

Often, companies market products in a vacuum. Inventors invent. Strategic planners plan. Focus groups focus. But in most cases, no one is certain how consumers will respond to a new product or service. Telemarketing enables sellers to gain immediate feedback from potential customers. Sales objections can be identified. Missing features can be determined. Competitive advantages and disadvantages can be uncovered. Market research and product promotion can be accomplished in one call.

## FLEXIBILITY

### Compete with the big boys.

Because a human being is delivering the sales message, telemarketing can customize the message to fit the exact needs and concerns of each buyer, unlike other forms of marketing, which present a static message to all.

Furthermore, telemarketing can *originate* from any location and *reach* any location with equal speed. Prospects who are too far away to be visited can be called.

When establishing retail locations is impractical, an office with a telephone can deliver the same message at a fraction of the cost. The phone is a great equalizer. Smaller companies can compete with mega-corporations. Local enterprises can reach national audiences.

## COST EFFECTIVENESS

### Improve return on investment.

Every advertising method contends that it is the most cost-effective approach, measured by whatever criteria most benefit that medium. In my mind, the only valid criterion for measuring cost-effectiveness is how many dollars it takes to generate a sale.

Unlike some media (e.g., newspapers and magazines) that brag about vague benefits such as "name recognition," the value of telemarketing can be measured objectively. Simply divide the revenue gained by the cost expended to calculate your return on investment (ROI). Admittedly, the calculation becomes more complicated when telemarketing is only part of the sales process or when the sales cycle extends well beyond the time when the calls were actually made.

In my experience, telemarketing is the most cost-effective way to reach and motivate targeted prospects. Mass media works best for mass audiences. But when success depends on reaching a relatively small group of isolated decision makers, nothing beats a professional caller who can weave through the maze of advertising cacophony and reach buyers the old fashioned way: one at a time.

# CHAPTER THREE

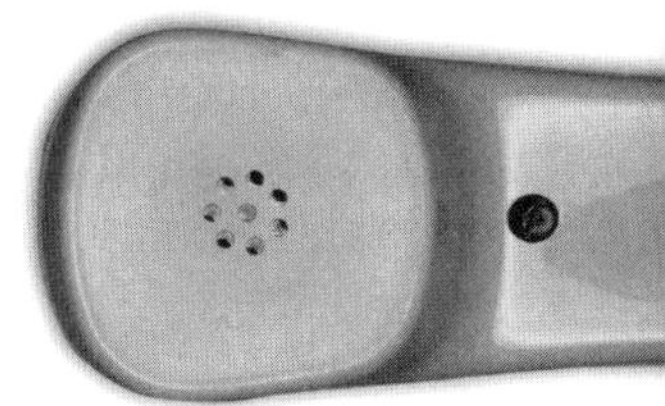

# Your mission, should you choose to accept it

For many, the term *telemarketing* invokes a visceral image of fast-talking con artists in smoke-filled rooms selling swamp land to sweet old ladies, or dizzy-headed high school dropouts reading phone scripts while you're trying to eat dinner. To combat the stereotype, business-to-business (B2B) practitioners now call themselves *telesales* or *inside sales* reps. Of course, a pig is still a pig no matter how sweet he smells. The issue is not what you're called, but what you do with that powerful tool called the telephone. I use the term *telemarketing* to refer to any sales activity conducted over the phone.

## EVOLUTION

### Do what technology cannot.

Changes in the marketplace have dramatically altered the role of B2B telemarketing:

*Long-distance rates*—The charge for nonlocal calls on a landline has fallen from 20 cents per minute to zero. Paying a small flat fee per month, companies can now make unlimited long-distance calls for free and afford to market their goods to anyone anywhere.

*Online purchases*—According to the Direct Marketing Association, online purchases are skyrocketing while purchases initiated by outbound calls are sinking to new lows. The company that used to buy its office supplies from a high school grad calling for a local vendor, for example, now orders everything online from a mega-store website. As a result of the proliferation of online commerce, human beings are less necessary in selling commodity goods.

*Technology*—Today's business products are becoming increasingly more technical and computer driven. Nothing is simple anymore. New technological gizmos require one-on-one demonstrations, and even mundane equipment is rarely self-explanatory. Consequently, more personal attention must be given to consumers.

*Do not call*—While the federal law prohibiting unsolicited sales calls does not regulate B2B calls (except in a few rare exceptions), it affects all telephone commerce. Telemarketers must be more sensitive to those they call, lest they be labeled as public nuisances and reported to consumer agencies.

In summary, the cost of B2B telemarketing has gone down, but the role of the caller has become more complex, requiring greater finesse and skill than ever before. Today's successful telemarketer must do what technology cannot do: establish personal connections, explain complex products, and engage the buyer in a consultative sales process.

## SPECIFIC ROLES

### Find your niche.

*Research*—Outbound calling can be effective in conducting market research. For example, one of my clients had developed technology that could personalize the colors and images of a website to fit each specific visitor. The developers were unsure who might buy the technology but thought it might be helpful to those who create websites. My job was to call several hundred webmasters, give them a conceptual overview of the technology, and ask whether they thought it might be helpful. They weren't interested, and the client directed its marketing attention elsewhere.

Telephone research can also be helpful in identifying contact information. Another one of my clients planned to mail a $500 marketing kit to the product managers of selected prescription drugs. My job was to contact the pharmaceutical companies who produce these drugs and determine the name and address of each manager. Considering that drug manufacturers are exceedingly hush-hush about their employees, I couldn't get an employee directory commercially or online. Instead, I started with the receptionists and progressed from employee to employee, asking questions for five weeks, until I had identified the right people.

Don't pretend to be conducting research when you're really trying to sell. On several occasions, I've been asked to "survey" decision makers about their equipment, processes, problems, and plans. Under the guise of asking objective questions, this technique is really designed to identify what prospects will buy and how much they'll pay for it. Some people call this "consultative selling." I call it self-defeating manipulation. For starters, the decision maker knows what you're trying to do from the outset and resents being treated like a no-brain pawn. In addition, no responsible business leader is going to spill his guts about corporate secrets to a stranger on the phone.

However, I have found that some decision makers are surprisingly willing to answer polite, nonintrusive calls about their business processes and needs. The key is to start with simple nonthreatening questions and move to more in-depth inquiries as the client allows. For example, if you're selling delivery services to companies that currently have their own delivery trucks and crews, you might start by saying, "The rising cost of gas has affected everybody. Has this been a problem for you?" With a little luck, the VIP will not only answer "Yes" but also offer more detailed information such as, "We've had to cut back on our delivery areas to cut costs." That's your opening to discuss the advantages of outsourcing deliveries to your company.

*Event promotion*—When a company invites prospects/customers to a special event (such as a meeting, webinar, or conference call), a telemarketer may call the invitees to remind them about the event and determine how many people will be attending. Based on my personal experience, most of the invitees won't remember ever receiving the initial invitation. Therefore, the follow-up call requires both an overview of the event and a second, more personal, invitation. In my experience, follow-up calls can significantly increase attendance at a marketing event.

*Lead qualification*—Prospects who visit a company's website or respond to other forms of marketing need follow-up calls. A telemarketer can answer any questions they may have, broaden their understanding of the product, and enable them to establish a connection with a live human being. The process also allows the company to further qualify each prospect based on interest, budget, decision-making authority, or other criterion.

In larger organizations, where sales and marketing exist as separate entities, telemarketing can serve as an essential link between the two functions. In a typical situation, the marketing department identifies prospects who have come to the company's website looking for product information and forwards these leads to the sales department.

Inevitably, problems arise in this process. Marketing may refer leads to sales that are not adequately qualified; that is, unlikely to actually buy. And sales reps may ignore referrals believing they are unqualified, which may or may not be true. As long as the company is making money, these problems are relatively invisible. But when revenue falls short of expectation, that's when the finger pointing starts.

In this scenario, everyone loses—the company and potential customers. Telemarketing can serve as a powerful bridge between all the parties, separating hot leads from tire-kickers and enabling time-strapped outside reps to focus their attention on those most likely to buy.

*Lead generation*—Most of my telemarketing has been "cold calling," that is, contacting new prospects who have not previously shown interest in a product or service. Generating leads by cold calling is the focus of this book. As explained in later chapters, the process involves five basic steps:

Organization—Setting goals and timetables, determining your target market, identifying decision makers, compiling a comprehensive and clean prospect database, learning all the basics about your product, and preparing scripts and collateral materials.

Access—Obtaining direct phone numbers and maneuvering past gatekeepers.

Delivery—Introducing yourself and your product to the decision maker, asking and answering questions, overcoming objections, and closing.

Record keeping—Maintaining accurate and current records of contact activities.

Follow-up—Maintaining ongoing contacts with

prospects in order to generate sufficient interest in your product.

Lead generation is a carefully orchestrated process that requires preparation, precision, and persistence. Every step must be executed with skill and professional passion in order to be successful.

As an old friend once told me, even a blind hog will find an acorn sometimes. Incompetent telemarketers will inevitably stumble upon interested prospects. Unfortunately, they'll also trample lots of other good leads as they root around.

As a professional telemarketer, I know that a few prospects will be immediately interested in my pitch and that a sizable percentage will never be interested. Like politicians on election day, my goal is to convert the undecided into believers. These are the ones who need my solution but don't know it yet. These are the ones who are open to a better idea if someone will turn on the light for them. These are the ones who typically reject the average telemarketer, not for the inferiority of his product, but for the inadequacy of his delivery. When these folks hear an irritating voice or an insincere-sounding pitch, they stop listening before the inferior caller has delivered the punch line. When they hear my voice, they are more likely to interrupt the chaos of their work world and consider my message.

*Direct selling*—While the role of direct B2B sales by phone is shrinking, opportunities still exist, particularly in promoting items that require customization or a one-on-one personal explanation, such as moderately priced software, printing, and advertising. Direct telephone selling is also particularly effective for selling upgrades and new features to existing customers, even when the unit price may be substantial.

## FOR BEST RESULTS

### Sell complex, higher-priced, value-driven products.

Telemarketing can be used to promote virtually any product or service. But in my experience, you can expect the best results when the product is complex and has a higher price, when the selling advantage is more value driven than price driven, and when access to the decision maker is severely limited.

*Complex products*—Impersonal marketing (such as direct mail, the Internet, etc.) is efficient when the product or service is already well understood by consumers. But when you're selling a new product or one that is so complex as to require a detailed explanation, such as software or insurance, telemarketing makes sense.

*Higher-priced*—Generally, the more expensive the item, the more necessary is human interaction with the consumer. For example, very few people buy houses or expensive manufacturing equipment sight-unseen. Telemarketing provides that human touch when face-to-face interaction is not possible or economically feasible. Therefore, telemarketing is often used to establish an initial personal relationship with the buyer, followed by a face-to-face appointment by a sales rep.

*Value-driven*—Telemarketing is more effective in promoting value-driven sales propositions than promoting price-driven ones. If the only difference between your product and a competitor's is price, traditional advertising is a more efficient way to promote your lower price. But when you're selling more subjective advantages, such as increased efficiency, time-savings, or superior service after the sale, you need someone to discuss these less tangible issues with the consumer.

*Limited access to decision maker*—Sometimes the only way to get your sales message to business decision makers is to call them on the phone. When they don't read your direct mail pieces, answer your e-mails, visit your website, or respond to your other advances, your best shot is telemarketing.

# CHAPTER FOUR

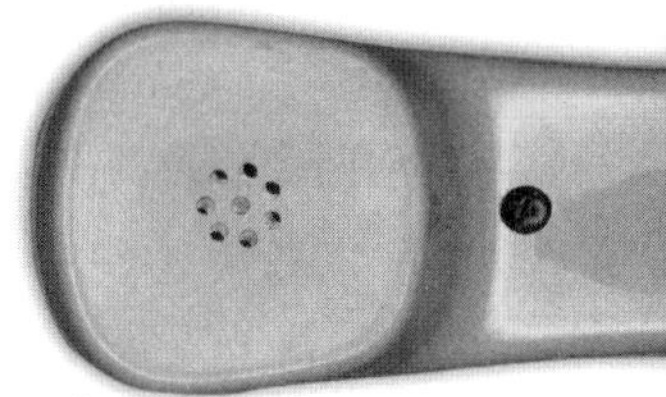

# Houston, we have a problem!

OFTEN, YOU'LL HEAR BUSINESSPEOPLE SAY that they've tried telemarketing, but it just didn't work. I don't doubt it. As explained in this book, identifying the right people to call, reaching them on the phone, saying the right words in the right way, and following up thoroughly and consistently is critical to success. Folks who sit down and make a few random calls from time to time are likely to be disappointed.

Telemarketing failures can generally be traced to three basic problems: uncertain goals, an inefficient system, and inadequate effort.

## NAVIGATIONAL ERROR

### Don't try digging to China.

I start every new job with the expectation that my employer knows what he's selling and who he's selling it to. That seems reasonable, but it is not always the case. I have spent hundreds of hours twiddling my thumbs while top level managers decide whether to sell product A or B. In other cases where the product is clear, the target audience is not. I'm asked to test this prospect group against that one, like an infantryman charging one new hill after another, trying to determine which direction draws the least enemy fire. In this kind of corporate chaos, even the most brilliant telemarketer is likely to fail.

A common conclusion about telemarketing is that it's all a numbers game. So is digging to China. True, ten people can dig ten times faster than one. But even with a million diggers, nobody is going to pop his/her head up in Beijing anytime soon. Simply moving in the wrong direction faster won't get you to your destination.

The more defined your target is, the more likely you are to hit it. I had a client once whose target market totaled 90,000 companies. That's not a target; that's a blur in the distance. While it would appear that having such a large number of potential prospects would increase the chances of success, the fact is that the more limited and more well defined the prospect audience, the more focus you can bring to the task, and the better results you will have.

The retail marketplace reflects the realization that nobody, including Wal-Mart, can sell everything to everybody. Profitable retailers are working harder and harder to define and attract their niche customers. Those who fail to find their place in the marketplace will find themselves in bankruptcy.

This approach is driven by two realities: (1) Limited resources. The larger your target audience, the greater the resources necessary to reach this audience. No one has an unlimited advertising budget, and no one can afford for the cost of sales to consistently exceed the profits realized. (2) Self-centeredness. Consumers want to believe that a company meets their particular needs. When the seller tries to appeal to too many target groups at once, each group feels slighted. Like mixing all the colors in one pallet, the end result is mud. No one is satisfied. Everyone walks away.

Confusion also arises concerning the role and strategy that telephone sales should take. Department heads typically disagree about whether outbound calling is a sales or a marketing function. Some believe that outside reps should do their own prospecting, while others believe in a two-step lead qualification process using an inside group. Often there are disagreements about when a lead becomes sufficiently qualified to be transitioned to an outside person. Confusion abounds regarding how much time a telemarketer should spend making phone calls and how much time he should spend identifying, organizing, and following up on leads.

Needless to say, it's hard to reach your destination if you can't agree on where you're going and how you're going to get there.

## SYSTEM FAILURE

### Make sure you're firing on all cylinders.

A successful telemarketing program operates like an efficient machine, processing raw materials (prospects) into finished goods (customers). As explained in this book, the system includes several important subsystems:

1. *Prioritization*—All leads are not created equal, and no one can perform more than one task simultaneously. Time is money. Businesses always prefer cash sooner than later. All these factors necessitate the identification of the best leads and calling them first.
2. *Message*—Saying the right words at the right time obviously affects the outcome of any conversation.
3. *Delivery*—How you say something is, in fact, even more important than what you say.
4. *Follow-up*—Most successful outcomes require repeated calls and other follow-up measures such as sending literature.

These steps should be conducted in a precise and timely manner in order to be most effective.

How many times has NASA canceled a launch due to some tiny malfunction? When prioritization, message content, message delivery, or follow-up malfunctions, results suffer.

## FUEL SHORTAGE

### Persist for as long as it takes.

No matter how well an audience is targeted or how efficiently a calling system is designed, nothing happens unless human beings actually make a sufficient number of dials. Like the lazy fisherman who packs his gear after an unproductive hour of casting, callers who make a few unsuccessful calls a day are never going to land the big one. Minute after minute, hour after hour, day after day, persistence pays.

If you call ten people and no one buys, should you quit calling? If no one buys after one hundred calls or one thousand calls, should you quit then? There's an old saying that "You shouldn't quit before the miracle happens." That's certainly the case in telemarketing. Most callers quit before they realize the value of their efforts.

# PART 2

# SELLING 101

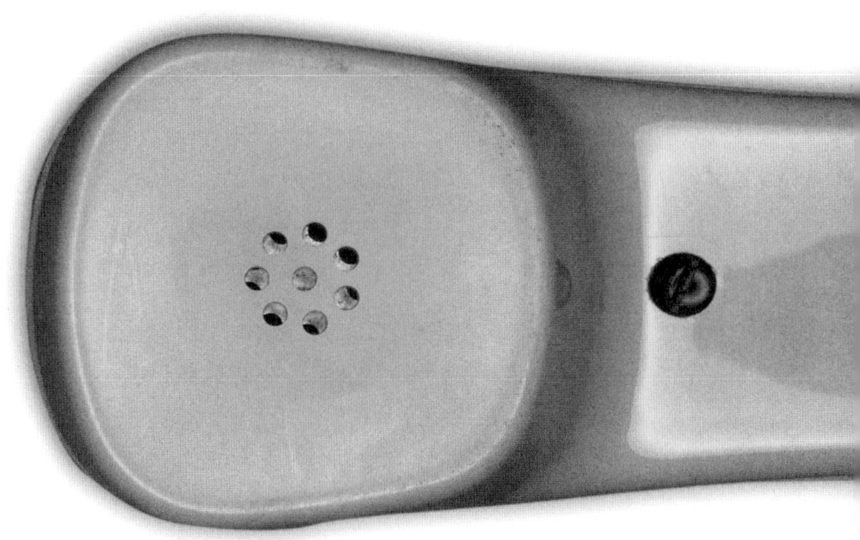

# CHAPTER FIVE

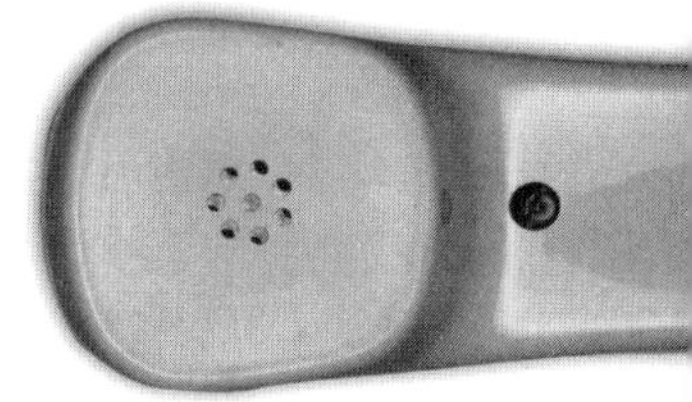

# The dancing refrigerator

People buy a product because it benefits them in some way; that is, it fills a need or solves a problem. People don't buy ice cream because it's cold. They buy it because it tastes good. That's the difference between a feature and a benefit. What something does is a *feature*. How something helps is a *benefit*.

Let's say that, after years of trial and error, you invent a dancing refrigerator. Yes, your incredible gizmo is amazing to watch. No, there's never been anything like it before. But in the end, who cares? Who is going to actually buy one? Yes, there are always a few folks who will buy anything new just to say they're on the cutting edge. But what about the mass market? Do you really see a rush to Best Buy for a Frigidaire that can move like Fred Astaire?

The problem is simple. While your product may be interesting, it's not useful. While it may be unique, it's not helpful.

The telemarketer's job is to explain why a given product will help the person being called. Will it save money for the customer or increase revenue? Will it increase efficiency within his operation or decrease regulatory violations? Will it make the buyer richer? safer? healthier? happier?

You may have a perfect script delivered in a perfect way, with perfect literature as follow-up, but you won't sell a thing if your product doesn't fulfill a customer need.

In order to convincingly position the benefits of your product, it's helpful to consider general benefits needed by all organizations and individuals.

> "Motivation is the art of getting people to do what you want them to do because they want to do it."
>
> —Dwight D. Eisenhower

## ORGANIZATIONAL BENEFITS

### Explain how the company will win.

Organizations have certain needs designed to ensure their survival and success. These include:

1. *Profit*—Anything that increases revenue or reduces cost is good. Profit is king. Lower costs can be accomplished by buying essential products/services at a lower price or by increasing output without increasing expenses; that is, greater efficiency. Increased revenue can be accomplished by increasing the number of sales or the average revenue generated from each sale. If you sell a product or service that increases profit (after the cost of your item is factored in), decision makers will listen.
2. *Constituency service*—Some organizations such as hospitals, schools, and governmental entities exist to serve their patients, students, citizenry, and so forth. Products or services that benefit these constituencies (make patients healthier quicker, improve student test scores, etc.) are recognized as beneficial.

3. *Employee satisfaction*—Every organization must maintain some level of employee satisfaction in order to remain in operation. Unhappy employees quit or find ways to waste time and money on the job. Companies that depend on scarcely available, highly skilled employees are particularly sensitive to the needs of their workers. For example, hospitals buy high-tech equipment, not only to benefit their patients, but also to keep their best doctors happy. Software design firms offer a dazzling array of on-site benefits, such as health spas, childcare, and gourmet cafeterias, to attract and maintain the best programmers. If you sell a product or service that increases employee productivity or decreases employee turnover, you're offering a true organizational benefit.
4. *Regulatory compliance*—All organizations must comply with certain local, state, and federal regulations. For example, everybody has to file a tax return and pay the required taxes. Many human resource functions (such as hiring/firing and benefits administration) are subject to government regulations. And that's just for starters. Every industry has laws, regulations, and standards. Products or services that educate organizations regarding regulatory compliance and offer more efficient ways to meet regulations (software, safety equipment, etc.), or assist firms that have violated regulations, will be perceived as beneficial.

## INDIVIDUAL BENEFITS

### Explain how the decision maker will win.

Understanding organizational benefits is just the beginning. Organizations don't buy products. People do.

Theoretically, the needs of an organization and the needs of the individuals who work there should be synonymous. In fact, people want to satisfy their own needs in addition to (or perhaps in spite of) the organization's needs. For example, decision makers, fearful that an initiative may reflect badly on them personally, may be unwilling to buy a new product. On the other hand, buyers whose departments are performing poorly may welcome something new as a way to improve their job security. Therefore, in order to determine the true benefits of your product or service, it is essential to determine both the needs of the organization *and* the needs of the decision maker(s). The telemarketer's job is to create and deliver a message that addresses both types of benefits.

Geoff Ayling in *Rapid Response Advertising* offers fifty reasons why individuals buy:

1. To make more money, even though it can't buy happiness
2. To become more comfortable, even a bit more
3. To attract praise, because almost everybody loves it
4. To increase enjoyment of life, of business, of virtually anything
5. To possess things of beauty, because they nourish the soul
6. To avoid criticism, which nobody wants
7. To make their work easier, a constant need to many people
8. To speed up their work, because people know that time is precious
9. To keep up with the Joneses; there are Joneses in everybody's lives
10. To feel opulent, a rare but valid reason to make a purchase
11. To look younger due to the reverence placed upon youthfulness
12. To become more efficient, because efficiency saves time

13. To buy friendship; I didn't know it's for sale, but it often is
14. To avoid effort, because nobody loves to work too hard
15. To escape or avoid pain, which is an easy path to making a sale
16. To protect their possessions, because they worked hard to get them
17. To be in style, because few people enjoy being out of style
18. To avoid trouble, because trouble is never a joy
19. To access opportunities, because they open the doors to good things
20. To express love, one of the noblest reasons to make any purchase
21. To be entertained, because entertainment is usually fun
22. To be organized, because order makes lives simpler
23. To feel safe, because security is a basic human need
24. To conserve energy, their own or their planet's sources of energy
25. To be accepted, because that means security as well as love
26. To save time, because they know time is more valuable than money
27. To become more fit and healthy; seems to me that's an easy sale
28. To attract the opposite sex; never undermine the power of love
29. To protect their family, tapping into another basic human need
30. To emulate others, because the world is teeming with role models
31. To protect their reputation, because they worked hard to build it

32. To feel superior, which is why status symbols are sought after
33. To be trendy, because they know their friends will notice
34. To be excited, because people need excitement in a humdrum life
35. To communicate better, because they want to be understood
36. To preserve the environment, giving rise to cause-related marketing
37. To satisfy an impulse, a basic reason behind a multitude of purchases
38. To save money, the most important reason to 14 percent of the population
39. To be cleaner, because unclean often goes with unhealthy and unloved
40. To be popular, because inclusion beats exclusion every time
41. To gratify curiosity; it killed the cat but motivates the sale
42. To satisfy their appetite, because hunger is not a good thing
43. To be individual; because all of us are, and some of us need assurance
44. To escape stress; need I explain?
45. To gain convenience, because simplicity makes life easier
46. To be informed, because it's no joy to be perceived as ignorant
47. To give to others, another way you can nourish your soul
48. To feel younger, because that equates with vitality and energy

49. To pursue a hobby, because all work and no play etc., etc., etc.
50. To leave a legacy, because that's a way to live forever

## RELATIVE VALUE

### Forgive those who cannot see.

The critical point to remember about selling benefits is that value, like beauty, is in the eye of the beholder. What one person sees as beneficial may be vastly different from what another person in a similar role in a similar company may perceive as beneficial.

The differences illustrate the emotional and intellectual complexity of human beings. Businesspeople like to pretend that their decisions are based on logic, not emotion. The truth is that none of us can completely separate one from the other. What we perceive as truth is ultimately based on our experiences in life and our emotional make-up. Schizophrenics who hear voices are certain of the reality of these voices. People who don't hear the voices are certain that they don't exist. After a decision maker assesses the "facts" of a purchase—for example, the price, the seller's reputation, the features of the product—the final decision comes down to subjective—that is, emotional—factors.

My last car-buying experience illustrates the point. I knew the model I wanted and wasn't interested in considering anything else. I knew the price I could afford (actually the payments I could afford) and wouldn't consider anything less expensive. I wasn't interested in shopping around and wanted to drive a shiny new something off the lot that very afternoon. I was a sales guy's dream.

The only thing left to do was close the deal. After test-driving the low- and medium-range versions, I was introduced to the deluxe model. As the sales guy droned on about engine performance and gas mileage, I was fascinated by the leather seats and the CD player. When he got to those features, my heart starting beating faster, and I exclaimed, "I love this car!" He immediately popped the question. Sixty minutes later I was cruising down the boulevard in my brand new chariot, hunkered down in my leather seat, listening to my favorite song on that super-cool CD player.

While I understand sales rejection objectively, I'm still amazed—subjectively—when a sales prospect fails to appreciate the value of my offering. My first thought is, "Why are you so stupid? Don't you see how much this will help you? Don't you realize that the benefits far exceed the cost?" All I can do is shake my head and say a prayer for those who fail to see what I see so clearly.

> "Customers usually buy on impulse, not logic. They base their buying decision on how they feel about a product or service. Get them excited about using your product or service, and you'll increase your sales."
>
> —Bob Leduc

# CHAPTER SIX

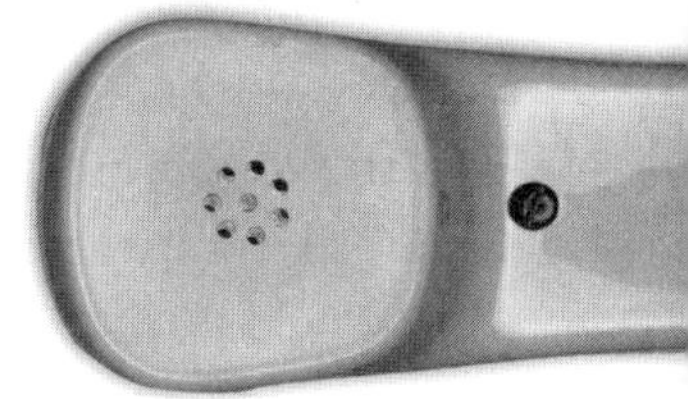

# Trust makes the world go 'round

ULTIMATELY, ALL HUMAN RELATIONSHIPS DEPEND on trust. Democratic government depends on the trust of the people. The monetary system depends on trust in the value of currency. Personal relationships depend on trust between the partners.

Business relationships would be impossible without trust. Lawyers like to think that contracts can spell out every contingency in such a way that trust is unnecessary. But dotting every "i" and crossing every "t" doesn't ensure that one party or the other will actually perform exactly as specified. Borrowers legally obligate themselves to repay debt, but they can still walk away from their obligations. Sellers promise guarantees which they may or may not be able, or willing, to keep.

In the end, buyers buy from companies they trust and from people they trust. In the end, no one purchasing a product can know as much about it as the seller. In the end, no one can count on a written contract to cover every contingency in every circumstance, or guarantee that all parties interpret every word in exactly the same way. In the end, the buyer must accept a certain degree of vulnerability and take a "leap of faith" into the arms of the seller.

Trusting requires both an intellectual and emotional judgment, a determination by the decision maker that (1) the facts add up and that (2) he/she has a good gut-level feeling about the matter in question. Trusting requires a calculated risk based on assessment of the odds for success, blending what you know about the past with what you speculate about the future.

Buyers tend to make trust judgments relatively quickly and rely on them for the duration of the business relationship. Trust lost is rarely regained. No matter how great your product is or how charming you are as a salesperson, a decision maker who does not trust your company in general, or you in particular, will not buy your wares.

## TRUST-BASED SELLING

### Build great relationships.

Several sales experts use the term *trust-based selling* to characterize the unique characteristics of selling based on trust.

According to Tony Alessandra (*6 Rules of High Trust Selling*):

"High trust selling begins with a mindset of a commitment to the long term. Today's customers buy differently, so today's salespeople must sell differently. Customers know that there is no urgency to buy; because good deals, good salespeople, and good companies come along every day. Price is less of an issue, because buyers are not just interested in great deals. They want great relationships."

Alessandra reminds us that the purpose of selling is not to gain revenue but to meet the needs of the client. When we're focused on giving (helping the client solve his/her business problems) instead of taking (getting as much money from the client as quickly as possible), then win-win outcomes occur; and long-term sales relationships evolve.

## BARRIERS TO TRUST

### Rebuild trust by being trustworthy.

We are all products of our experiences and carry baggage from traumatic events of the past into our relationships in the present. Business relationships are no exception. Some decision makers may stubbornly resist trusting you and your company due to previous experiences having nothing to do with you.

While you may never know the root cause of this resistance, Drs. James and Constance Messina tell us that people who have trouble trusting share certain key attitudes:

1. I have been hurt too much in the past, and I refuse to be hurt again!
2. As soon as you let your guard down, you will be stepped on again!
3. No one is to be trusted!
4. I get no respect from anyone!
5. Everyone is out to get me!
6. You can never let your guard down because all hell will break loose!
7. Everyone is out to get as much as they can out of you!

It's impossible to imagine all the frightening experiences of those we call, all the events that have damaged each individual's ability and willingness to trust both in his/her personal life and in business relationships. We like to think that we are calling into a blank slate. We like to assume that the person answering the phone will judge us on our behavior and not some hidden preconceived cancerous feelings locked deep inside his/her psyche.

Unfortunately, that's just a fairy tale. If your voice sounds like the voice of someone who has previously lied or cheated, no amount of persuasion is likely to convince the prospect that you can be trusted. This isn't a conscious decision on the part of the individual, or necessarily one that he/she wants to make, but a subliminal instantaneous defense mechanism hot-wired into the person's decision-making process, grounded in the instinctual desire to escape danger.

Considering that many of us have experienced trust-busting experiences, it might seem impossible that human beings would ever trust each other. True, some don't. But many of us do. It's a testament to the enduring human spirit that we can overcome adversity and thrive. Children from abusive homes can grow up to become great parents. Rape victims can find safety with loving partners. Divorced people can start over in new, more trustworthy marriages. Thankfully, many of us whose trust has been violated in the past discover that, over time, our desire to connect with other people overcomes our fears.

I was asked recently whether I am optimistic about life, considering both my advanced age (well, not that advanced!) and my years of cold calling. I immediately answered, "Yes! I couldn't do this work otherwise." In examining my feelings on the subject, I realize that a significant part of my hopeful outlook in business derives from the fact that so many people I call are friendly and interested in establishing a trusting—albeit short-term—relationship with me. I find that honesty breeds openness and that being trustworthy leads others to be trusting.

"Internalize the Golden Rule of sales that says: 'All things being equal, people will do business with, and refer business to, those people they know, like, and trust.'"

—Bob Burg

# CHAPTER SEVEN

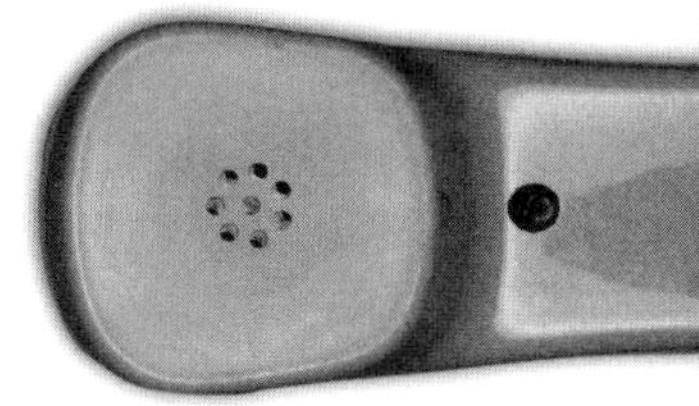

# Can your company be trusted?

Before a consumer will buy, he/she must trust you and your company. Outlined below are factors that influence the likelihood that your company will be trusted.

## OLD FRIENDS ARE THE BEST FRIENDS

### Cherish your existing customers.

A buyer is much more likely to purchase from a company with whom he/she has previously done business than with a new seller, assuming that the previous sales experience was positive. Repeat customers are the best customers. This reminds us to take care of our existing customers before worrying about getting new ones. Considering the cost of sale associated with acquiring new business and the continuous threat from competitors, corporate survival often depends on keeping what you have. If you happen to call an existing customer who has a complaint, stop selling and start repairing the damage. Listen carefully. Identify the problem. Reassure the complainer. Immediately contact customer service within your organization about the issue. After a sufficient time, call again to inquire about resolution of the issue. If the problem has been resolved satisfactorily, you now have an inside track to the next sale.

## WILL YOU BE MY NEIGHBOR?

### Promote your proximity.

People are more likely to trust a company that is located nearby than one located far away. While the Internet has challenged this conclusion to some degree, consumers still make most purchases from local vendors. Trusting those nearby has been a common characteristic of human beings for eons, reflecting the fear of destruction from outsiders. If you are located a considerable distance from the person you're calling, reassure the customer that you are easy to reach and already working with other local companies (if you are).

## BIGGER IS BETTER, SOMETIMES

### Hype your size.

Except in cases where people have established long-term relationships with local mom-and-pop stores, most buyers would prefer to buy from a bigger company than a smaller one, believing that larger companies must have done something right to have grown to that size. This affinity reflects another instinctual predisposition for finding safety in numbers. Governments, political groups, religious organizations, and corporate conglomerates all appeal to our desire to belong and to be part of something bigger than we are.

If you're not big, praise yourself for being small. Emphasize personalized service, quick turnaround, and maximum flexibility—qualities that mega competitors cannot match.

## THE ESTABLISHMENT

### Make your age an asset.

People are more likely to buy from companies that have been in business longer. Again, the thinking is that a company that has existed for an extended period must be okay. When a business is sold, its value is determined not only by the market value of its tangible assets and receivables, but also by the company's goodwill, a subjective measure of its reputation calculated in dollars. If you've been in business five years or more and have a great reputation, flaunt it.

Ironically, consumers are always looking for something new and improved to replace the status quo. If you're a newcomer, promote your new ideas, your new products, and your new vision for the future. Appeal to the public perception that better things are being invented every day.

## THE WOW FACTOR

### Extol the extraordinary.

Some new products are so incredibly cool that you want to trust the seller, regardless of any other factors. The term "snake oil salesmen," synonymous with rip-off artists, originated with traveling sellers who peddled miraculous elixirs. A volunteer in the audience (planted by the peddler) with an apparent malady was suddenly cured after one sip of the magic liquid. Wow! Forget the fact that the seller was a stranger, that no one knew the actual contents of the potion, and that anybody with a formula that good would be living in a mansion somewhere and not grubbing from town to town in a broken-down wagon. Forget everything. Just buy it!

Telephone scammers use the same techniques. They call unsuspecting older folks, living at death's door, and offer them something so marvelous, so incredible that they're willing to send good faith money to a total stranger.

In the real world, "wow" products, such as the iPod, are rare. But even though your widget may not cure cancer or otherwise revolutionize life as we know it, don't forget that people still want to hear about great things. Despite their skepticism, they're still willing to listen to a better idea. They're still waiting for that magic elixir that will cure what ails them.

Tell them why your product is better. Tell them how they will finally find relief from a nagging problem they've been unable to solve. Tell them honestly. Tell them with enthusiasm. Make 'em say "Wow!"

> "People don't ask for facts in making up their minds. They would rather have one good, soul-satisfying emotion than a dozen facts."
>
> —Robert Keith Leavitt

# CHAPTER EIGHT

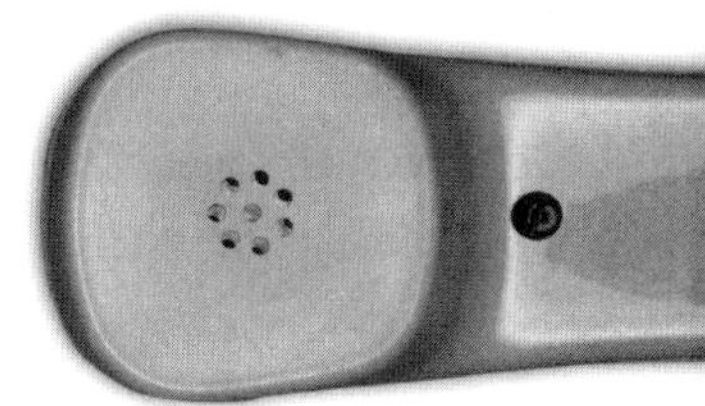

## Can you be trusted?

TRUST IN YOUR COMPANY IS not enough. The customer must trust you personally in order to buy. Here are keys to building that trust.

### I AM YOU, AND YOU ARE ME

#### Find something in common.

People are more likely to trust someone who seems similar than someone who seems different. The connection may be based on nationality, religion, race, gender, sexual orientation, geography, class, education, age, sports team favorites, or a myriad of other variables. The degree to which a given factor affects trust varies from person to person. Some people may not care about a caller's gender or race, but may be deeply affected by his politics or religion.

We can't change differences like race or gender, but we can focus on similarities that we may have with the person being called. Maybe you both like the same sports team. Maybe you both lived in the same part of the country or vacationed in the same place. Maybe you both have teenage children, served in the military, or have aging parents. Look for similarities and nourish them.

Listen to the values expressed by the customer. Maybe the person says something about hating companies that don't deliver on their promises. You express your agreement. Now the two of you share a common value, a connection that is probably more important than other differences you may have.

## I LIKE; THEREFORE, I BUY

### Be a nice person.

People would rather buy from people they like than from people they don't. Faced with competitors on every corner offering virtually identical products and services, banks are now doing whatever they can to seem likeable. Gone are the days of the stern-faced money changer telling us that banking at his institution is a privilege. Today, the faces inside the typical neighborhood bank are smiling. (They don't call them "branches" anymore. Now they're "neighborhood banks.")

Tellers call you by name and offer punch and cookies. Today, the emotionless cash brokers want us to like them. Why? Because it's profitable, of course. They've discovered what everyone knows. We'll drive a little farther and pay a little more to shop with people we like.

*The Likeability Factor*, written by Tim Sanders, offers a fascinating litany of studies testifying to the power of being liked:

1. Doctors give more time to patients they like and less time to those they don't.
2. In civil legal proceedings, likeable clients are more likely to receive compensation than less likeable clients.
3. Gallup polls have found that, since 1960, likeability is

the only consistent predictor in presidential elections.
4. Easy-going, likeable people have one-half the divorce rate of the general population.
5. Deciding who stays and who goes in downsizing depends on how well people are liked by their supervisors.

So what makes a salesperson likeable? Is it all about jokes and stupid stories? Is it talking about sports teams and what the family's been doing lately? Does it require showering compliments and exaggerated claims of undying friendship?

While some likeable salespeople undoubtedly perform these routines, being liked in a business setting is best determined by how the seller feels about himself and his customers. A likeable person is happy and peaceful. He/she emits positive energy, constant optimism, and quiet reassurance. The likeable person is genuinely concerned about others, rejoices in their victories and mourns at their defeats. The likeable salesperson is more concerned with helping than selling, more concerned with doing the right thing than the expedient thing, more interested in long-term relationships than closing the sale today.

## STRAIGHT SHOOTERS

### Tell the truth.

No one trusts a liar. And since sales folks are assumed to be liars by many, telling the truth in sales situations is absolutely essential. If you say your device can do something, be completely sure that it can. If your company has been in business for four years, don't say five.

I'm reminded of an enthusiastic young job applicant who applied for a telemarketing position in my department. He had inside sales experience and seemed to be suited for the position. Unfortunately, his resume stated that he had a four-year college degree when, in fact, he had three years of college. When the lie was exposed, he was rejected for the position. Ironically, I didn't care whether he had a degree or not.

That's one of the problems with lies. Often you tell one to fix a problem that, in the end, doesn't need fixing—only to get canned later, not for the problem that worried you, but for the very act of lying. What a waste!

Presidents Nixon and Clinton were condemned more for their lies than their actions. Corporate crooks, like Ken Lay, were convicted more for false statements than direct theft. Play it straight. Tell the truth.

But what about the issue of completeness, telling the *whole* truth and nothing but the truth? How much information is too much information? When is withholding information the same as lying?

While this issue is certainly one for personal moral interpretation, I would suggest a few guidelines when deciding how much to say:

Describe every fact related to the safety of the product. The tobacco companies were prosecuted not because they sold a deadly product, but because they failed to inform the public that it was a deadly product. For the sake of technical liability and personal ethics, disclose all significant facts related to health and safety.

Describe any significant limitations or problems with the product. Better to admit these openly and explain the circumstances early than have them discovered later. Public-relations experts say that you should "get in front of a story," telling your version of the facts before someone else can. In the long run, this minimizes the emotional impact of the problem and solidifies your position as an honest salesperson.

Answer all questions completely. If a buyer asks whether your product will perform XYZ function, explain precisely and completely to what degree the product will perform this function.

> "As you travel down life's highway, whatever your goal, you cannot sell a doughnut without acknowledging the hole."
>
> —Harold J. Shayler

## WISE GUYS

### Be smart without being a smart-ass.

Smart people are generally held in high regard unless they try to lord their intelligence over the rest of us. In school, we tended to respect the smart kids in the class, but not the ones that raised their hands and tried to answer every question the teacher asked. In selling, as in school, the key to being respected for your intelligence is to be smart without being a smart-ass.

To gain the trust of the buyer, the seller must know all the facts about the product for sale and be able to articulate those facts in a clear, coherent manner. The decision maker wants to hear just enough technical jargon to reassure himself that you know what you're talking about. Too many scientific terms and ten-dollar words imply that you're talking down to the person. Vague, simplistic language makes you sound stupid or implies that you think the buyer is stupid.

## HEAR ME, HEAL ME

### Listen to what people are really saying.

Ironically, in generating trust by phone, what you don't say is often more important than what you do. Anybody can talk. Gab, gab, gab. That's what the buyer expects you to do. And a certain degree of it is necessary.

The power play, however, is listening. The more you listen, the more the buyer believes that you care, that you'd rather help meet a need than just close a sale. Giving someone your time and attention is a precious gift, one that most folks seldom receive. Giving engenders trusting. As you listen more to the buyer, the person will begin listening more and more to you.

> "Knowing when to keep your mouth shut is invariably more important than opening it at the right time."
>
> —Malcolm Forbes

## A HELPING PROFESSION

### Give and you shall receive.

People have a way of knowing whether you actually care about them or not. Maybe their perception is based on how long you listen, how many approvals you express, or how warm your voice sounds. Maybe it's a vibe that travels through the phone line. Regardless, they know, or at least think they do. Yes, some callers are such good liars on the phone that they can fool the folks they call . . . but not many. Unfortunately, the opposite is more likely to be true. Telemarketers who may genuinely care are too often judged as uncaring due to the way they sound on the phone.

The best way to convince someone that you care is to act that way. Listen to what the person is actually saying, not just what you want to hear. Ask questions to gain understanding, not to manipulate. Acknowledge the person's pain without immediately trying to fix it. Suggest solutions that may actually help, not just ones that lead to a sale. Don't argue or criticize. Praise honestly and often. Respect the person's time and point of view. Take "no" for an answer.

In the short run, this golden rule approach might actually produce fewer sales. There are always a few customers who can be maneuvered into buying things that aren't in their best interest. But in the long run, the person who cares makes more sales that the person who doesn't. Maybe the buyer is choosing between your product and a cheaper one sold by a grab-and-run sales jockey. The odds are that you'll get the business and will continue to get it, sale after sale.

The other benefit of giving more than you take in a sales situation is that you can relax. You have nothing to fear. You won't get caught with your hand in the cookie jar, because you're ensuring that the customer gets a cookie too.

## CELEBRITY SELLS

### Look as pretty as you can.

We are all attracted to celebrities, particularly the rich, famous, and beautiful. We're surrounded by their images everyday. Commercials tell us that, if we buy this or that, we'll be a celebrity too. Perhaps it is our inherent unhappiness at life's mundane nature that compels us to ogle jealously at the stars. Or maybe the sight of beautiful people is simply a form of harmless entertainment.

Regardless of the reason, celebrity sells. Beauty sells. Success sells. Accordingly, communicate the best image possible of your company, your product, and yourself. If your firm is the market leader, say so boldly and often. Ensure that your company website is striking, colorful, and memorable. Only send literature that is professionally and attractively prepared. And make sure that you always sound professional and intelligent on the phone, without background noises or poor technical connections.

One of the wonderful aspects of telemarketing is that the listener cannot see you. As the phone-sex industry has proven, we tend to believe that a person's body looks as good as he/she sounds. If you sound attractive, the customer is likely to believe that you look attractive. And whether a preference for beautiful people is right or wrong, it's still a reality. The more beautiful you sound, the more influence you'll have.

> "The philosophy behind advertising is based on an old observation that every man is really two men—the man he is and the man he wants to be."
>
> —William Feather

## I BELIEVE IN YOU AND ME

### Don't worry. Be happy.

We all prefer to be around folks who are confident, not the arrogant "I'm better than you" types, but the "I'm happy to be me" types. In a business setting, where pressures are constant, pitfalls are many, and the strong routinely overpower the weak, decision makers are drawn to those who seem to know what they're doing. When an indecisive, stuttering telemarketer calls, the buyer instinctively says, "How do you expect me to believe in your product when you don't even believe in yourself?"

When you sound afraid, the listener subconsciously thinks that you have something to hide. When you sound confident, the buyer thinks you're probably telling the truth.

Selling on the phone can be scary. You're calling strangers who are already skeptical. You're afraid of saying the wrong thing and sounding stupid. You're afraid some jerk is going to chew you out and hang up in your face. You're afraid you'll get fired for doing a bad job. You're afraid that everybody will find out how afraid you really are.

Like Franklin D. Roosevelt once said, "The only thing we have to fear is fear itself." To sound confident, you have to take the pressure off yourself. Remember, you're doing the best you can. Remember, you're telling the truth. Remember, you're trying to help the customer, not hurt him. Remember, no matter what happens on this call, you're still an honest, caring person who will survive no matter what.

> "Remember, your customers don't buy your product. They buy you."
>
> —Alfred E. Lyon

# CHAPTER NINE

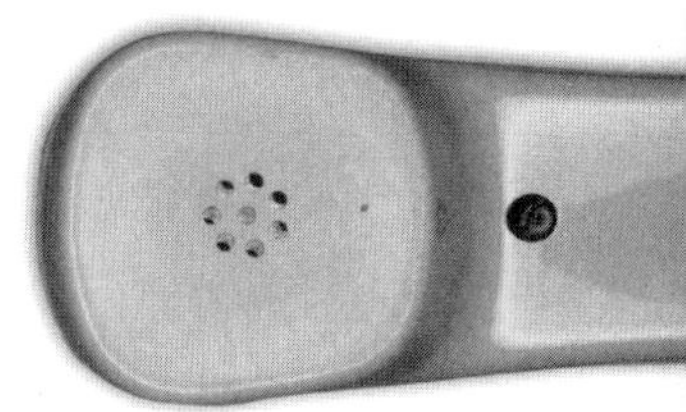

# Event-driven marketing

IT HAPPENS ALL THE TIME. You've given a great presentation, asked the right questions, and received the right answers. The decision maker has already said that he likes your product, and he seems to like you. Apparently, based on the conversation, price and budget are nonissues. The moment has arrived, that dramatic all important moment when you ask for the sale. You're relaxed as the words flow confidently from your lips, because you're sure that you're going to hear "Yes!"

Instead, the decision maker says "NO!"—not because your product is inferior, or because a competitor got the biz, or because money is a problem. In fact, the guy has lots of positive things to say about what you're selling.

No, the problem is timing. The buyer has other priorities right now. His plate is full. Something old must be completed before something new can be attempted. He has bigger fish to fry. Not today. Maybe later. Maybe next year. He can't make any commitments right now.

And that, as Hamlet reminds us, is the rub. It's not enough to sell your product. You must sell it now. In sales, as in most things except horseshoes and hand grenades, close doesn't count. You can't deposit "laters" in the bank.

Of course, if the decision maker is willing to establish a firm sale date in the future, that's almost as good as a sale now. Everything has a sales cycle, and pricier items always take longer to close. But in most circumstances, the buyer who says he'll consider your product later is simply telling you "no" in a less definite way.

The truth is that most of us buy things based on short-term needs. We're planning a trip, so we buy luggage. The kids are going back to school, so we buy fall clothes. We're redecorating the den, so we buy new furniture. Events trigger our decisions to buy now.

The same is true for business purchases. Corporate VIPs are much more likely to buy what they need (or at least think they need) now than to buy what they might need later. Budgets are limited. Staff members are overworked. Deadlines are looming. Vision is increasingly short-term, focused on immediate profits and immediate problem solving.

Therefore, pitch your products to companies that have an immediate need for them.

So how do you know what a particular company needs? One way is to ask probing questions during the conversation that lead the decision maker to explain his/her needs. We'll discuss these kinds of questions later in the book. You can also uncover a company's immediate needs by researching public records found on the Internet and in newspapers, magazines, association newsletters, and similar sources.

## ORGANIZATIONAL CHANGES

### Ride the whirlwind.

Businesses, like people, are in a continual state of flux. Employees come and go. Products are added and deleted.

Locations change. Leaders change. Companies make money and lose money. Investors invest, and creditors withdraw. Lawsuits are won and lost. Firms merge together and break apart.

In each organizational change, there is a sales opportunity, a need that calls out for satisfaction. The more you know about the changes within an organization and the sooner you learn it, the more likely you are to be selling just the right product at just the right time.

Unless you know somebody who knows somebody, your source of information about organizational changes is likely to be a newspaper, business publication, or website—all public documents. In your research, try to determine when a particular change actually took place. For example, new employee announcements are generally within thirty to sixty days after the person begins working. By contrast, mergers of privately owned companies are typically completed months before they are announced. (Publicly traded companies are subject to strict rules governing the release of information.) New products are usually in the production pipeline for years before they're released.

Unfortunately, you can never be sure of the current status of an organizational change at the moment you learn about it. For example, if you manage commercial real estate, you'd be excited to learn about a merger of two in-town companies, since they are likely to be looking for a single larger space in which to consolidate operations. However, you may find that this decision was already made months before you learned of the event. Don't despair. For every ten announced mergers, the odds are that at least one is still looking for more space.

Organizational changes are like drying clothes. All the

various elements are tumbling around and around as the water slowly evaporates. There's always a degree of uncertainty and chaos in the process. Ideas are tried, discarded, and replaced with new ones. Priorities change. People change. Immediate plans become long-term, and vice versa. The twisting and turning continues until all the water is gone and all the details are finalized. Your best course as a salesperson is to jump into the mix, connect with the decision makers, and ride the whirlwind until the machine stops.

## MARKET TRENDS

### Help them succeed.

As the old saying goes, the only constant in this world is change, particularly in the business world. Companies that anticipate the future succeed. Those who ride the wave survive. Those who refuse to change wipe out on the beach.

One critical variable shaping the world's markets are demographics. In the United States, for example, the Baby Boomers are placing an unprecedented demand on medical care. Worldwide, China has become a major economic player as services such as telephone customer service and computer programming are being exported overseas. These examples are among the most obvious. But every industry is experiencing trends in the marketplace, forcing changes in product design, customer targeting, and, ultimately, in every aspect of operations.

I once sold software that enabled physicians to access their patient data on PDAs, such as Palm Pilots and Blackberrys. When our company started, few individuals owned these kinds of devices; Therefore, demand for the access software was low. Within five years, 100 percent of hospital residents and 60 percent of all physicians owned PDAs. What a difference! Hospital CIOs, who had originally refused to consider our product citing physician disinterest, began to return my phone calls in response to doctors' inquiries.

By contrast, I also worked for a $100 million company that woke up one morning to find that the hardware they had been selling for $30,000 could be replaced for $100 by competitors. Like surfers with broken noses, they had blindly ridden the same old wave until it suddenly disappeared beneath them.

Successful companies anticipate and shape the future. They can foresee the next steps in technology and anticipate emerging needs that will explode in the not-too-distant future. They are ahead of their time, but not too far ahead.

If you're selling a cutting-edge product, identify the industry leaders who have already demonstrated a willingness to innovate, and try to understand what they're striving to accomplish. Position your product as a way to make those visions come true sooner, simpler, and/or at a lower cost.

If you're selling an improvement on old technology, assure the decision maker that you respect his history and want to help him be even more successful in the future. Show the noninnovator how he can move forward without abandoning his traditions and without leaping headlong into an unknown future.

> "Two shoe salesmen found themselves in a rustic part of Africa.
> The first salesman wired back to his office:
> 'There is no prospect of sales. No one here wears shoes!'
> The other salesman wired:
> 'No one wears shoes here.
> We can dominate the market. Send all possible stock.'"
>
> —Akio Morita

## COMPETITION

### Keep them in the game.

Nothing motivates buyers like the fear of competition. The store owner who is perfectly happy to operate business as usual, year after year, suddenly wants to redecorate, restock, and reprice when a similar shop opens around the corner. While competitive forces are often cruel and unfair, they force changes in the marketplace that create selling opportunities.

When I was selling hospital software, I often focused on physicians we called *splitters*, doctors with admitting privileges at more than one hospital in the same geographical area. The most important splitters were cardiologists, since they generated more revenue for a hospital than other specialists. Using this approach, I would contact these VIP physicians and interest them in our product, particularly by focusing on our software's benefits to cardiologists in other areas. Armed with the support of one or two key heart doctors, I then played one hospital against another, telling administrators that their most productive practitioners were likely to operate more often in the hospital with the best technology, that is, our technology. Faced with losing their best revenue generators to competing facilities, I always got a return call from key decision makers. To cap the deal, my sales manager would sometimes add a noncompete clause, agreeing to refrain from selling our solution to a competing facility.

Another strategy is to identify companies that already have similar capabilities as those offered by your product and convincing their competitors that they must match these capabilities in order to survive and thrive. This approach focuses on the followers in the marketplace who don't care about being ahead, but loath being behind. These are the companies that, often wisely, wait for larger, better funded, risk takers to test the latest gizmo and work out the bugs before adopting the improved version.

Playing the competition card requires a degree of finesse. At the heart of the message is fear—a fear that you will be gobbled up by the competitive monster unless you buy what I'm selling. Overtly trying to scare people about impending doom may work for backroom con artists selling security systems to old ladies, but subtlety is the order of the day in informing savvy business decision makers about a problem.

For example, instead of saying, "Your business will be in serious trouble if you don't do what your competitors are doing," try "I don't need to tell you that you're in a highly competitive market. To maintain your advantage, you may want to consider my product."

Imagine that the person you're calling is standing on the edge of a cliff. One wrong move and this confident-sounding three-piece suit will be just another pile of mush on the rocks of commerce below. Your approach is slow and deliberate; your voice is calm and reassuring. You don't shout out, "Hey Joe! Watch out for that next step. It's a doozie!" Instead, quietly and confidently, you tell the cliff-hanger that you recognize his dilemma and that you're there to help.

## COST INCREASES

### Show how spending saves.

The skyrocketing price of fuel illustrates how cost increases can cascade across industries. Transportation becomes more expensive, making local production more valuable and distant production more expensive. Plastic, created from oil, costs more, making virtually every product cost more.

Tourist locations have fewer visitors. People spend less for nonessential items, because they spend more for an essential item, gasoline. More corn is used for gasoline supplements, increasing its price and, therefore, increasing prices for beef producers that depend on corn for cattle feed.

Whenever the cost of business increases dramatically and consistently—whether due to increased fuel prices, labor costs, construction costs, taxes, and so on—sales opportunities exist. Anything that reduces the usage of higher-priced items, or reduces the cost of other essential items, is going to be popular. If you're selling something whose return-on-investment is significant and can be realized in a relatively short period of time, decision makers will be happy to take your calls.

## NEW REGULATIONS

### Sell compliance.

New federal, state, county, and city regulations create new business opportunities to interpret, document, and implement these regulations. For example, tax laws offering credits for environmentally friendly construction have led to a demand for "green" products and the expertise to use them. When HIPPA (Health Information Portability Protection Act) regulations were enacted, one of my clients contracted with a large insurance company to automate the distribution and maintenance of HIPPA compliance forms. Recently, the Supreme Court ruled that carbon dioxide emissions are legally considered pollutants and can be regulated by the Environmental Protection Agency. No doubt, telemarketers selling pollution solutions are hard at work.

Of particular value from a sales perspective are new laws and regulations that set deadlines for compliance. For example, if safety regulations require that each factory worker in a given industry wear a particular piece of equipment by a given date, sellers of that equipment will have a field day in the quarter preceding the deadline.

Typically, those affected by new laws and requirements fit into four categories: (1) immediate compliers who are constantly aware of regulatory changes and have time and resources to act before they are required to do so; (2) compliers who fall in line slowly over time; (3) last-minute compliers who move begrudgingly and slowly to meet the deadline; and (4) noncompliers who simply ignore the regulations until they get caught.

Like fishing, sales opportunities exist with all groups. If you're the first guy with a line in the water, you'll get the early risers. If you can fish all day, you'll catch a bucket full. But if you can find the watering hole where all the big ones are looking for one last snack before dark, you'll be reeling them in with both hands.

And the fish that don't bite? Just wait. The ones that don't float by upside down will be begging for your help sooner or later.

## DISASTERS

### Educate without terrifying.

Companies that have experienced a recent disaster, such as fire, flood, or wind damage, are looking for ways to rebuild economically, insure their property in the future, and secure their assets. In the computer world, hackers pose the greatest threats. Information technology leaders who have experienced significant data loss or security breaches will be looking for better ways to identify system vulnerabilities and destroy intrusive programs.

However, most sales opportunities are not with those who have experienced an actual disaster, but with similar companies who are afraid of suffering the same fate. The insurance industry thrives on this concept. They're not peddling policies to the guy whose house just burned down, but to his neighbors and his neighbor's neighbors.

Products that prevent, mitigate, or repair disaster damage will always be popular. The key is to help the consumer understand and appreciate the threat. A manufacturer without safety problems may not appreciate the potential damage of chemical spills until informed about a little-publicized disaster at a similar facility. In this sense, the seller's role is to educate, not to terrify; to act as an informed friend, not as a salivating vulture.

# PART 3

# THE RIGHT COMPANIES

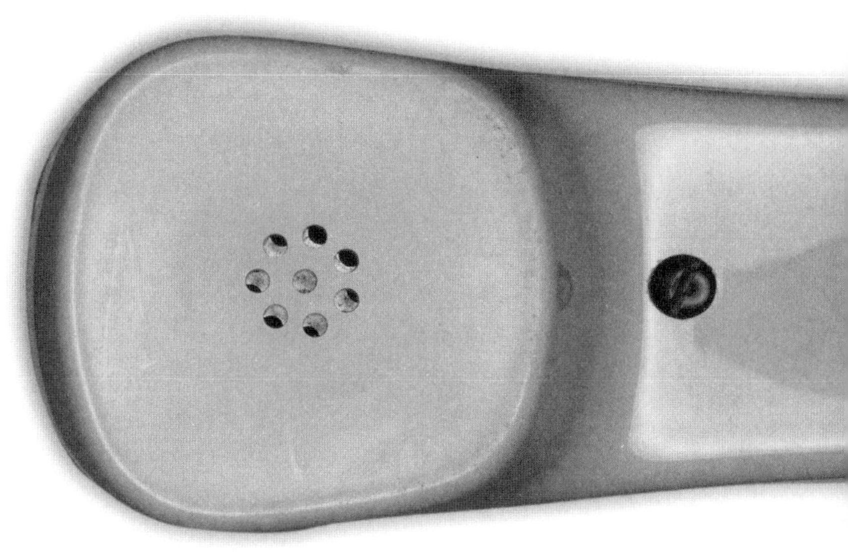

# CHAPTER TEN

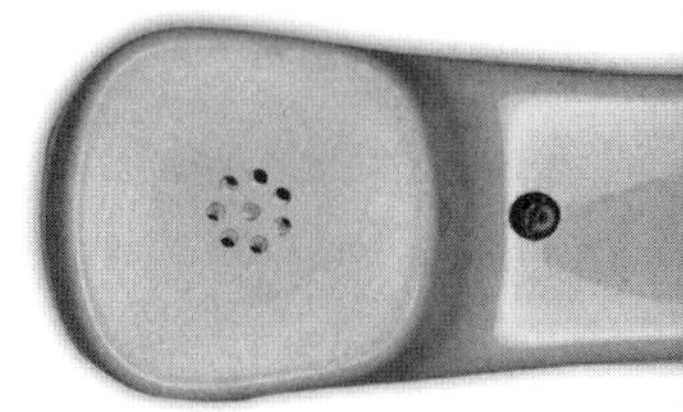

## The case of Big Bob

One day, Big Bob looked out of his window at Big Bob's Office Equipment Emporium in Raleigh, North Carolina, and decided that he was going to sell more copy machines than anyone else in America. Since he'd built his business on personal contacts, he determined that telemarketing was the best way to sell his products. So he called his wife's cousin, Eddie "Gift-of-Gab" Mahoney, and hired him as the company's first and only telephone inside sales business developer (TISBD).

The next morning, Big Bob and Eddie met to plan the campaign. "Who do you want me to call, cous'?" Eddie asked, sipping his coffee. "Everybody!" answered Big Bob without hesitation. "Every business in America. And I want it done fast. Let me know after lunch how long it'll take."

That afternoon, the two world-shakers looked at the numbers. First, they discovered that twenty-four million businesses exist in the United States. Then, after practicing their telephone routine, they determined that a hardworking telemarketer could make a maximum of twenty calls an hour, assuming that the caller had a preprinted call list and that he was able to actually talk with a business decision maker 15 percent of the time. After allowing for meetings, personal calls, lunch, and coffee breaks, they figured that Eddie would actually be on the phone six hours a day or thirty hours a week. Calling twenty prospects per hour, he could then call a total of six hundred potential buyers a week or 2,400 a month. After dividing the total number of businesses by the number of calls per month, they calculated that Eddie would be finished in 10,000 months or about 833 years. Even at a modest fee of $10.00 an hour, Eddie was excited about the $16.8 million he'd be earning for the work. He could send his wife on that round-the-world cruise she'd always wanted and finally have some peace and quiet.

Big Bob was upset. He couldn't afford to wait eight centuries to be rich and famous. Big thinker that he was, Bob began to imagine lots of Eddies on the payroll, a whole stable of telemarketers dialing for dollars. What if he hired ten people to make calls? That would reduce the time to eighty-three years—still not soon enough. Maybe a hundred, he thought. Then he'd be rich in only eight years, and still young enough to enjoy it. Things were looking great!

So BB (as his friends like to call him) went to his favorite hometown banker and asked for a small business loan to get things rolling. "How much ya' need?" asked Friendly Frank, the bank manager. "Well, I'm expanding my business and want to put a few folks on the telephone to sell my copy machines," replied Big Bob. "I figure that if I had enough money to carry everything for the first year, I'd be in good shape." "No problem," Frank grinned. "How many new employees do you need?" "A hundred," said Bob. "At $10 an hour, plus $10 for benefits, they'll only cost me about $2.2 million. Buying equipment and phone service will be another $2 million, plus renting a new building for them all will be about 60 grand. With incidentals, I'd say $5 million will probably do the trick."

After scribbling all the numbers down furiously on an official looking form, Friendly Frank looked up and asked the $5 million question: "What collateral do you have?" Apparently, a "great idea" was the wrong answer; and Bob slowly dragged his disappointed self back to his office, angry that, once again, his American dream had been thwarted by reality.

On some level, we're all like Big Bob, full of ambition, driven by dreams of prosperity on the battlefield of free enterprise, challenged by the reality of limited resources and limited time.

They say that telemarketing is all about the numbers. That's true, but not in the sense that calling more prospects necessarily leads to more sales.

Imagine that you have two jars of marbles. Jar A has nineteen red marbles and one green one. Jar B has nineteen green marbles and one red one. If your objective is to find a green marble, then you're obviously better off reaching into Jar B, where you'll find one after the first or second try; and you'll find nineteen after twenty tries (95 percent). With Jar A, the odds of getting a green marble are only one in twenty (5 percent), and it might take you twenty draws to find it.

After exactly the same amount of effort, the person dipping into Jar B will be nineteen times more successful than the poor soul reaching into Jar A.

You would think that savvy business types would understand and appreciate such a simple idea. But in my experience, suggesting call preparation to most employers is like suggesting that you get paid for nothing. "We hired you to call, not to think!"

The key to successful telemarketing is figuring out which jar has the most green marbles, calling those companies that are the most likely to buy, sooner than later.

In one of my favorite jokes, the airline pilot comes on the intercom and says: “I have good news and bad news. The bad news is that we’re totally lost. The good news is that we’re making great time!”

Telemarketing that fails to identify the most likely buyers may be making great time and still be totally lost. No matter how hard you try, you’re never going to get there. Like Big Bob, who wants to call every business in America, you’ll be dead long before your objective is reached.

# CHAPTER ELEVEN

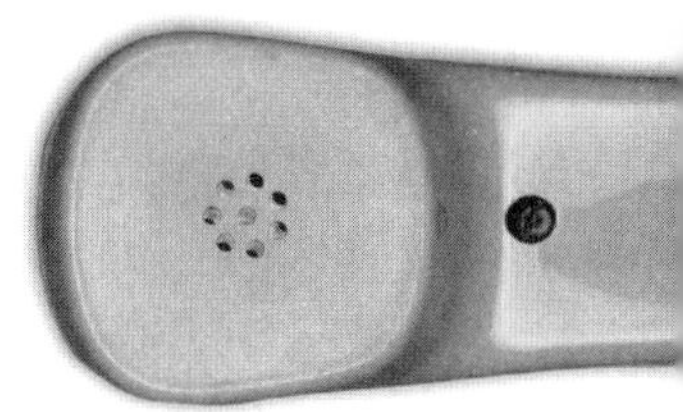

## Target marketing

THE FIRST STEP IN IDENTIFYING target companies is to know your existing customers. They say that those who ignore history are bound to repeat it. In sales, failing to understand what has come before condemns you to reinventing the wheel, learning again what works and doesn't work, which type of companies like your products and why. If you have been in business for a year or more, you can appreciate the cost in time and money already invested in market research. So in determining who to call, start with companies that most closely resemble your existing customers.

But if you are a new company or selling a new product or trying to reach a different segment of the marketplace, you won't have history as a guide. At this stage, larger sellers turn to sophisticated market research programs, using surveys and focus groups to evaluate who is most likely to buy. Smaller firms can use the same techniques on a smaller scale, making selected calls to potential target groups to test the waters.

Regardless of size, some business executives use their gut-level instincts to determine who to target. Those whose instincts turn out to be right, like Steve Jobs and Bill Gates, are hailed as business geniuses. The bad guessers land in the corporate junk pile.

## LOCATION

### Name the neighborhood.

One of Big Bob's options is to sell closer to home. Using a sophisticated national database firm like InfoUSA, it's possible to narrow a prospect list geographically based on state, standard metropolitan statistical area (SMSA), county, city, and within a specified radius of your location.

For those who are unfamiliar, a SMSA is a group of counties, defined by the Census Bureau, that represents a general marketplace for local consumers. For example, Bob's store is located in the Wake-Durham County SMSA. For more information about SMSAs go to
http://www.census.gov/population/www/estimates/aboutmetro.html
http://www.census.gov/population/estimates/metrocity/80mfips.txt

Using data from the Census Bureau and other sources, you can target companies based on average income, median education level, and other demographics in a given location. For example, maybe you're a wholesaler selling high-end watches. You might want to target stores located in high-income neighborhoods. Or perhaps you buy and sell commercial space in several states. Using population records, you can identify cities and zip codes where unusual growth is taking place and where, consequently, there may be more commercial builders who might be interested in your properties. For more details about available census data, go to:
http://quickfacts.census.gov/qfd/.

In Bob's case, he decided to focus on his home county (Wake) that has a total of 33,444 businesses.

## ORGANIZATION

### Select the structure.

You may want to target companies based on whether they are corporations, partnerships, or sole proprietors. For example, of the 24 million businesses in the United States, 18.6 million do not have employees—the companies are actually individuals. Of the remaining firms, 4.4 million are legal corporations, and the balance, partnerships. If you're selling self-employment insurance, you'll want to focus on sole proprietors. If you're a corporate tax attorney, you'll want incorporated prospects.

## SIZE

### Total the employees.

If you're selling multitasking software for human resource (HR) departments, you'll probably be more interested in companies with larger numbers of employees, companies that perform a myriad of HR processes. On the other hand, if you're selling do-it-yourself business planning software, you'll be more interested in smaller firms. In the case of Big Bob, he's interested in companies that can afford his copy machines but aren't already entangled with national suppliers. Consequently, he decides to target companies that have at least ten employees, but not more than fifty, located in his county. His revised call list now has 6,375 records.

## REVENUE

### Count the dollars.

It's also possible to identify companies based on their annual revenue. Admittedly, this process is based on estimation, since actual tax records are not in the public domain. The figures are based on actual earnings reports released by public corporations, industry averages calculated by trade groups, and surveys conducted by census takers.

In most cases, the amount of income is directly proportionate to the number of employees. As one increases, so does the other. But some industries generate more money per employee than others. For example, a brokerage firm or a mortgage company is likely to earn more revenue with fewer employees than a manufacturing firm.

## YEARS IN BUSINESS

### Add the age.

Firms selling basic business products and services often target new companies, figuring that they'll need office space, computers, furniture, copiers, business cards, copiers, and other equipment. These start-ups can be identified from list brokers or by studying public records such as new corporation listings and business license applications.

As someone who has both sold such lists and made calls into them, new businesses are rarely good prospects for several reasons. First, they're usually cash poor, operating from home on a shoestring budget. Whatever money they have goes to keeping their lights on. Also, many of these start-ups aren't operating companies at all. Maybe they were started for ego satisfaction. Maybe they're real estate trusts created to buy and sell property. And finally, many of the "new" businesses identified by public records aren't new at all. They've been operating, maybe for years, and have finally decided to buy a business license or to incorporate.

As a result of these limitations, your company may only be

interested in companies that have actually operated for a minimum period of time. List brokers like InfoUSA can select business records based on years in business.

Having already experienced painful incidents with new companies, Big Bob decides to limit his telemarketing campaign to firms that have been in business for at least two years, reducing his total call list to 5,910 records.

## NATURE OF BUSINESS

### Pick the product or service.

You may want to target prospects based on what they sell or do. List brokers can select companies based on their (1) industry grouping, or (2) standard industrial code.

Industry groups are as follows:

1. Retail
2. Services
3. Transportation
4. Finance, insurance, real estate
5. Wholesale/distributors
6. Manufacturing
7. Construction
8. Agriculture/forestry/fishing
9. Mining
10. Public administration
11. Not classified

Within each grouping are subgroupings that become more and more detailed until all products and services are assigned a specific number called its standard industrial code (SIC). For example, a shoe store has the SIC of 5661. For a full listing of all codes, go to http://www.

osha.gov/pls/imis/sicsearch.html.

After repeated failures to sell copy machines to public entities, Big Bob has no interest in calling these types of organizations again, so he eliminates industry group 10. And he has never sold anything to farmers, foresters, fishermen, or miners, so he eliminates groups 8 and 9. That leaves him with a call list of 5,167.

## OTHER VARIABLES

### Consider all the options.

You may want to focus on certain types of professionals, for example, doctors, lawyers, engineers, CPAs, and architects. Besides list brokers, you can also obtain lists of professionals from public records, such as licensing boards, and from professional associations. For example, if you offer a medical coding service, you'll only be interested in physicians. Or like many stockbrokers, you may want to target all professionals.

List brokers can also select companies for a call list based on other factors such as

1. The company's credit rating
2. Estimated amount spent on phone book advertising
3. Public versus private companies
4. Profit versus nonprofit
5. Headquarters versus branch locations
6. Franchise or not
7. Whether the firm has a website

Two quick examples of how this data may be useful: At one time, I developed mailing lists of wealthy homeowners based on public property tax records and sold the data to a variety of companies who used it for advertising. Insurance agents were particularly interested. Over the years, I discovered that agents with full-page ads in the Yellow Pages were much less likely to buy than agents with bold single-line ads. Who would've thunk it?

On another occasion, I sold website design services. I found that companies with an existing website were much more likely to buy a new site than firms who had never had a site at all.

## EPILOGUE

### Start today.

As it turns out, BB and Eddie never got around to calling the 5,167 prospects on the list they bought. Their wives got so tired of waiting for the millions they were supposed to make that they took off for Miami in BB's Cadillac. After that, the boys spent so much time tilting long necks and feeling sorry for themselves that they never quite got around to picking up the phone. Maybe tomorrow . . .

# PART 4

## THE RIGHT PEOPLE

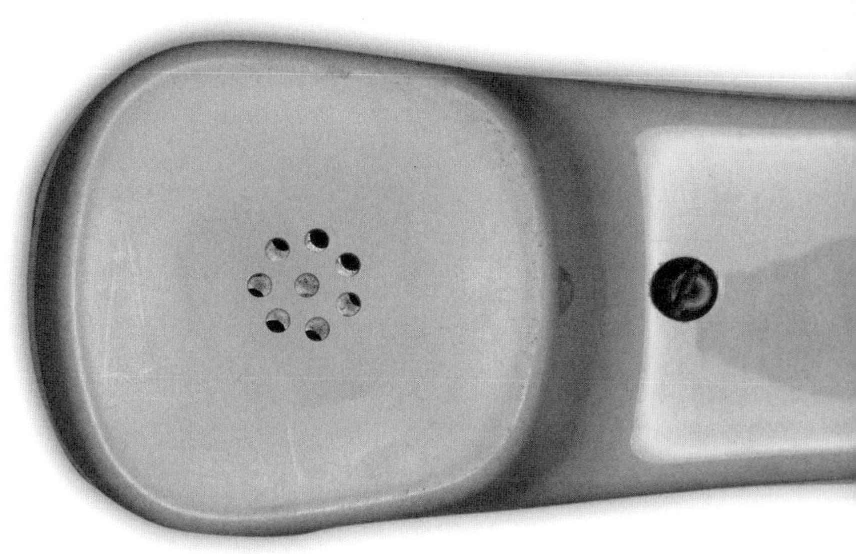

## CHAPTER TWELVE

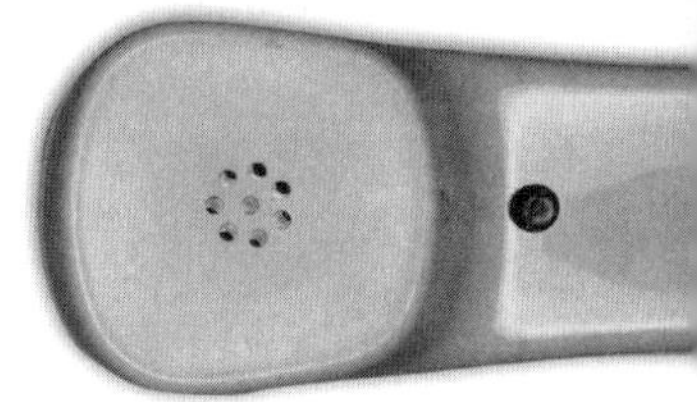

# A day in the life

THE BETTER YOU UNDERSTAND THE person hearing your message, the more likely you are to influence that person. This chapter and the two that follow are designed to offer insight into the typical business decision maker.

## BUSY

### Disturb at your own risk.

All decision makers are busy: talking with customers, managing employees, calculating budgets, evaluating new products, and most often, putting out fires. Needless to say, they're not waiting by the phone for a telemarketer to call. The last thing most of these folks want is a conversation with a stranger about a new product or service. Your call is an interruption, an intrusion, an aggravation in an already aggravating day.

Make your call as pleasant as possible, despite the initial reception you're likely to encounter. Your attitude must be positive; and your product, important. You're outside the buyer's closed door. If you're going to knock, you better have something important to say.

## STRESSED

### Think of yourself as an aspirin.

Remember that the decision maker is not busy having fun. You're not interrupting a party but an already stressful day. As President Truman so eloquently said in a plaque on his desk, "The buck stops here." The bigger the problem in an organization, the higher it rises. Supervisors and their supervisors get paid the big bucks, not for their brilliant ideas or sparkling personalities, but for their ability and willingness to solve problems. It's no surprise that a high proportion of business leaders have ulcers and heart attacks.

Into this pressure-cooker strolls the happy telemarketer, eager to please, carrying a magic product that will make all the company's troubles disappear. From a sales perspective, the fact that the buyer is stressed out is probably a good thing. The fact that he feels pain means that he wants relief. The greater the pain, the greater is the need for pain relief. Think of your call as an aspirin, not one more nail in the coffin.

## SKEPTICAL

### Turn on the lights.

Business decision makers are inherently skeptical. Survival in the corporate world requires caution, hoping for the best while anticipating the worst. Buyers share a common alma mater—the School of Hard Knocks. They've all made mistakes and suffered from the mistakes of others. They've all purchased products/services that didn't turn out as advertised. They've all had dashed hopes and career setbacks.

Then you call, full of sunshine and optimism, offering a solution that's the greatest thing since sliced bread. You're selling hope, a promise that things will be better later if the decision maker will buy something now. You're selling expectation, not reality; and that distinction is not lost on the buyer. He's been promised miracles before. Rarely, if ever, have the promises been fulfilled.

The successful telemarketer faces the skeptic unafraid, because he believes in his product. And more importantly, he believes in the benefit that the buyer will experience as a result of buying the product.

## HOPEFUL

### Fulfill a dream.

Despite the stress and doubts that dominate his world, the decision maker remains hopeful—hopeful that his problems have solutions, hopeful that his enterprise will prosper and grow despite all the obstacles. While some believe that cash is the engine of free enterprise, I contend that hope is ultimately more important. The American dream is that poor kids get rich, that victory springs from defeat, that adversity can be overcome.

So despite his problems and his skepticism, the decision maker subconsciously believes that, one day, things will get better, that somebody will deliver the solution he's been waiting for. That's the button that you want to push when you call. It's not about price or features or customer references. It's about solving problems for the buyer. In the end, it's all about hope.

## AMBITIOUS

### Support their journey.

Most are in leadership roles because they want to be. They like the power, the prestige, or simply the opportunity to create or achieve. They are typically reaching for something—more money, more accomplishments, more fame and fortune. Appeal to their ambition. Position your product as a way to solve a significant corporate problem or open an important new opportunity.

# CHAPTER THIRTEEN

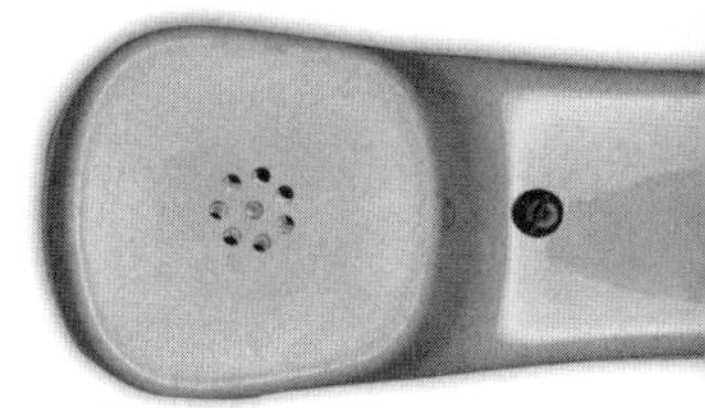

# You are what you do

A DECISION MAKER'S PERSPECTIVE ON you, your company, and your product is directly linked to that person's role within the organization.

## ENTREPRENEURS

### Let them have it their way.

People who create their own successful businesses are a special breed. First, they have enough insight to recognize an unfulfilled market need. Second, they are creative enough to visualize a new product or a new variation on an old product that will satisfy that need. Next, they are resourceful enough to gather the resources needed to produce and market their innovation. And finally, they are sufficiently organized and disciplined to manage the new enterprise in the real world of commerce.

Unfortunately, few entrepreneurs are good at all four abilities. Some create wondrous products that have no market demand. Some see the need but develop the wrong product. Some create products that address market needs but lack the resources to produce and sell them. And some have great products that satisfy market demand, plus lots of resources, but are poor managers.

Regardless of their strengths and weaknesses, people who create their own businesses are sure of one thing—they're right! They believe that, at least in their universe, they're smarter than everybody else. In this creative universe, the entrepreneur is god, breathing divine enlightenment into the dust of the old to engender a new living entity fashioned in his own likeness. Man, what an ego! (Takes one to know one!)

So in order to sell something to this person, you need to understand his vision and reinforce his goals. Explain how your product will bring success sooner and at a lower cost.

## SOLE-PROPRIETORS

### Help them stay in business.

Seventy-five percent of all the businesses in America are sole-proprietorships; that is, the one and only person working for the company is the owner. As my father would say, this person is the "chief cook and bottle-washer." Examples include beauticians, carpenters, insurance agents, accountants, lawyers, doctors, child care operators, retail store owners, artists, and similar professionals.

The primary concern of most sole-proprietors is survival. With the exception of certain professionals and well-established specialists, the person who owns and operates his own business is typically cash-poor, lacking capital reserves to grow or to weather unexpected shortfalls. In many cases, the business revenue supports the business and the owner's family. The owner is inevitably working long hours and making personal sacrifices for the enterprise.

So if you're calling a one-person shop, think price first. You may have the greatest product ever invented, but if it costs more than a few dollars, your call will be over before you know it. If you do close the sale, get cash up front. Sole-proprietors may have excellent intentions, but many have poor credit.

## CHIEF EXECUTIVE OFFICERS (CEOs)

### Produce results while minimizing risk.

In an organization with more than one employee, there is always a head honcho, also known as president, chief executive officer (CEO), executive director, or other title of high authority. The larger the organization, the less this person is involved in day-to-day details and the more he/she is involved in corporate strategy.

One responsibility of the CEO is to establish long-term goals for the organization, to determine where the enterprise will be in one year, five years, and ten years. Part of this mission is ensuring that the enterprise has a clear definition in the marketplace. Steve Jobs, CEO of Apple, has not only positioned his company as an industry leader in technology innovation, but has also introduced products that will define the marketplace for years to come.

The CEO is naturally concerned about profits, but may in fact be more interested in long-term market share than in short-term revenue. He/she is typically more focused on image and corporate reputation than on day-to-day operations.

Cold calling the CEO of a larger organization is a waste of time. As a telemarketer, you are unlikely to be offering anything that will shape the long-term reputation or market share of the enterprise. And the odds of directly reaching this person by phone are practically zero.

If you choose to call the CEO, plan on talking with his/her

secretary, who is a trusted gatekeeper on whom the decision maker relies. Briefly explain your proposition and ask whether you can send information to her that she can pass along. After you do, follow-up with the secretary to arrange a time when you can speak with the VIP.

## CHIEF FINANCIAL OFFICERS (CFOs)

### Make it add up.

The chief financial officer (CFO) is the head bean counter, the final authority on money in and money out. While this person may be included in long-term strategy discussions, he/she is more concerned about short-term realities like cash flow, revenue realization, and tax consequences. Unless you're selling accounting software, don't bother calling the CFO.

## CHIEF OPERATIONS OFFICERS (COOs)

### Help keep production humming.

A company's CEO needs someone to keep the lights on while he's looking at the big picture. That person is the chief operations officer (COO), responsible for keeping production running on time and under budget. The COO is a nuts-and-bolts person, more interested in increasing efficiency than planning long-term strategy, more interested in reducing costs than in increasing revenue, more interested in how something operates than in how it appears to the public.

If you're selling machines, software, or employee services that increase output without increasing cost, call the COO. Be prepared to explain your product's ROI (return on investment). Be ready to prove, in facts and figures, that buying your product now will generate a definable and reliable cost savings in the foreseeable future. (The quicker the return, the better.) Save your jargon and schmoozing for somebody else. The COO hasn't got time to waste on BS artists.

## CHIEF INFORMATION OFFICERS (CIOs)

### Sell simplicity.

The chief information officer (CIO) is the head computer geek, charged with the never-ending task of buying and maintaining hardware and software for the organization. Regardless of a company's long-term strategy, operational efficiency, profit margins, or sales and marketing campaigns, everything stops when the computers go down. And systems inevitably go down, all systems. While most employees work forty- or fifty-hour weeks, the CIO is on-call 24 hours a day, 7 days a week, 365 days a year.

Of all major officers within an organization, the CIO probably receives more sales calls than anyone else. Anybody with a computer product/service and a phone is dialing his number. While he's busying running from spot to spot trying to plug holes in the dyke, one nitwit after another is imploring him to drop everything and have a long chat about some new-fangled gizmo.

Ironically, the very technology that is supposed to make corporate life simpler only makes the CIO's life more complicated. Therefore, this executive is only interested in two objectives: (1) keeping the system running, and (2) making the IT world easier and quicker to manage.

Don't expect to reach the CIO directly by phone, and don't expect a call back unless the person is seriously interested. You'll have better luck calling a second-tier member of the information services staff. For example, if you're selling computer security, try the network security officer.

If you're selling telecommunication equipment, call the telecommunications specialist in the IT Department.

## SALES MANAGERS

### Show them the money.

The sales manager's only concern is generating revenue. This person believes in doing whatever it takes to close a deal. If a customer wants something he can't offer, he's likely to go to production and ask them to create it—or simply promise the customer first and inform production later.

Typically competitive and aggressive, the sales manager is surprisingly easy to interest in any revenue-enhancing product with particular interest in trade shows, prospect lists, sales training, and contact management software. While you're unlikely to reach the sales manager directly by phone, be assured that he/she listens to every voice-mail message, like an old lady at the slots, hoping that the next one will be the big payoff.

## MARKETING MANAGERS

### Prove your case.

Larger profit-making organizations tend to have marketing departments, responsible for company advertising. While both sales and marketing have the same final objective—generating revenue for the company—marketing is focused on issues such as public image, product education, and lead generation, while sales is focused on closing sales.

Marketing managers are much less optimistic, and much more skeptical, than sales managers. Generally, they are not interested in any idea which they did not personally think of themselves. They see themselves as social scientists basing their decisions on carefully analyzed empirical evidence derived from reliable sources like focus groups and market surveys. While this may be true in some cases, market managers are usually making educated guesses based on their gut-level feelings. I've heard people say that half of all advertising dollars are wasted. But unfortunately, no one—including the typical marketing manager—knows which half.

Even so, call these officers about any advertising opportunity. Pitch it in an objective-sounding manner with statistics about audience profile, response rates, and so forth. If you can't do that, just say that the company's competitors are advertising that way. Keeping up with the Joneses works in business just like it does in private life.

## PROFESSIONALS

### Respect their credentials.

Certain types of organizations have unique leadership positions. For example, hospitals typically have a head doctor who goes by the title of chief of staff or vice president of medical affairs. While this person may be a specialist in any medical field, he/she is generally responsible for representing the physicians' perspective to hospital administration, for ensuring that the hospital upholds quality standards, and for resolving interdepartmental medical issues. Like all physicians, the "head doc" is nearly impossible to reach directly by phone. Leave a message with his/her assistant, then send follow-up material by e-mail or snail mail.

Leaders in health, public accounting, law, architecture, and other professional fields share a common characteristic—they want to be respected for their professional status as measured by years of education completed, certifications or designations awarded, and recognized standing with colleagues. Their egos need to be stroked and their opinions valued. Expect their decision-making process to be long and punctuated with lots of meetings and fancy sounding recommendations. In the end, professionals tend to be indecisive buyers, apparently in order to avoid any mistake that might question their expertise.

## EDUCATIONAL LEADERS

### Wait for them to analyze.

On the surface, selling products to educational institutions, particularly colleges and universities, seems easy. The decision makers tend to be intelligent, reasonable people who can, theoretically, evaluate the pros and cons of your product logically and impartially. Schools of higher learning tend to have committees for every issue, staffed by experts, whose members can usually be identified by Internet research.

There's only one problem: analysis paralysis. (I didn't invent that term, but it certainly applies here.) These folks simply can't decide anything within any reasonable amount of time. Their analytical minds require a thorough review of all the literature and complete discussion by all participants. Eventually, their findings become a report that gathers dust on some administrator's shelf.

These kinds of people are too smart for their own good. They'd rather think than act. They'd rather do nothing than make a mistake. And in the end, they make poor sales prospects. If you've got lots of time and enjoy endless follow-up, this is the industry for you. Otherwise, keep moving.

## GOVERNMENT OFFICIALS

### Offer political cover.

Governmental organizations at all levels share certain common characteristics. First, the decision makers are generally paranoid about being criticized by the press and by those higher in the chain of command. While this fear is also present within profit-making enterprises, public entities are much more vulnerable to criticism. Every taxpayer feels that he/she has the right to know everything about every governmental decision and to criticize that decision as loudly as possible. Public decision makers, therefore, tend to move much more slowly in purchasing products and services. They have to be more careful than private enterprises about the prices they pay and the vendors they select. The process of buying becomes just as important as the product itself.

# CHAPTER FOURTEEN

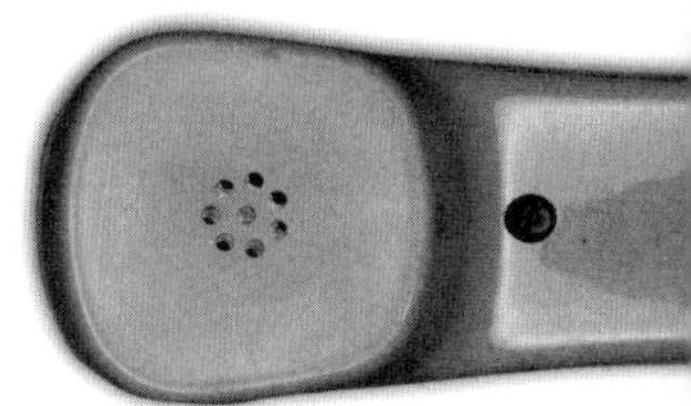

## Hot buttons

To BE TRULY SUCCESSFUL IN telemarketing, you need to know as much as you can about the individual you're calling. What are the decision maker's "hot buttons?" What business issues particularly concern him? What does he believe? What does he want to accomplish?

Imagine how easy selling would be if you could read the buyer's mind. You'd know exactly what to offer and exactly how to do it.

I've worked for several companies who wanted me to ask probing questions of the decision maker in order to uncover such detailed information. They want me to start with a question like, "What problems are you having with your computer security?" They think that the person on the other end of the phone, who doesn't know me from dirt and has a million other priorities, is going to pour out his heart with a long detailed list of all his problems so that I can then tell him how we, coincidentally, can solve all those problems. Wouldn't life be lovely if it worked this way?

In reality, the people you call are going to tell you very little, at least until they've spoken with you several times and have grown to trust you. Even then, they're hesitant to expose their weaknesses to anyone, especially a salesperson.

Instead, you need to identify the need before you call and offer a solution in the first thirty seconds of your call. You need to press a button in the listener's psyche that will open his mind to your presentation. The more accurately you can define that button, the more successful you'll be.

## NEWCOMERS

### Start early. Stay late.

A decision maker who has been hired recently is unlikely to make any significant change or purchase until he is better established within the new organization.

Start by examining the person's activities in his previous job. For example, if a CIO instituted wireless Internet connection throughout an institution in his previous job, he's likely to do the same in the new job.

Selling something to a new leader is usually a long-term proposition. Trying to reach this person directly in the first three months on the job is a waste of time and often counter-productive. Instead, introduce yourself to the leader's administrative assistant and then follow-up with a short personalized letter (and business card) congratulating the VIP on his new appointment. Ship the letter by second-day UPS/Fed Ex to the administrative assistant with a handwritten follow-up note asking her to forward your information to her boss. Call her the next day to confirm her receipt of the material.

A week later, call and ask her to schedule a five-minute phone call with Mr. Big so that you can introduce yourself. Make follow-up calls and send product news every thirty days thereafter until an appointment is set.

## OLD TIMERS

### Keep it the same, only better.

Typically, the longer someone has remained in a leadership role, the less likely that person is to institute new things. These people are usually set in their ways, convinced that they've considered all the products worth considering. Their approach is: "If it ain't broke, don't fix it."

The trick is to convince an old timer that (1) you admire the wonderfulness of his current operations, (2) you respect his undeniable wisdom, and (3) you want to help him be even more wonderful. Show this person how your product enhances the status quo without criticizing it, how it fits seamlessly into existing operations, and how it has proven itself in other well respected organizations. This decision maker thinks of himself as a member of an exclusive club of senior statesmen who are wiser than the rest of us. So if you have a large prestigious customer who is already successfully using your solution, drop the name. The old timer will pick it up in a hurry.

## PUBLIC FIGURES

### Promote their notoriety.

Decision makers who are regularly quoted in news stories and professional articles are more likely to want notoriety than less visible folks and more likely to be drawn to products and services that attest to their leadership. Therefore, if your customers include leaders in a given field, then the publicity prone VIP is likely to buy too in order to keep up with his peers.

Not only does this ambitious VIP want to lead, he wants to be seen doing it. For the public figure, achievement is hollow without publicity surrounding it. This person is ideal for cutting-edge technology or grandiose projects that have a high probability of success. (In the end, he would rather do nothing than risk his reputation on an unsuccessful project.)

Ask this kind of leader for his advice in evaluating your new product or service. Make him an advisor. Customize some small aspect of your product to fit his specific vision. After the sale, ensure that everything works perfectly. Then help him roll out the publicity machine to praise his (and your) brilliance.

## PET PROJECTS

### Pat the pet.

Determine a decision maker's priorities, particularly his/her pet projects, and position your product as something that will enhance that goal. If the person has publicly announced his intention to make his organization one of the best, explain how your product will enhance achievement of that goal. If the VIP intends to integrate multiple locations into a single IT and communications structure, position your wares as an essential ingredient.

# CHAPTER FIFTEEN

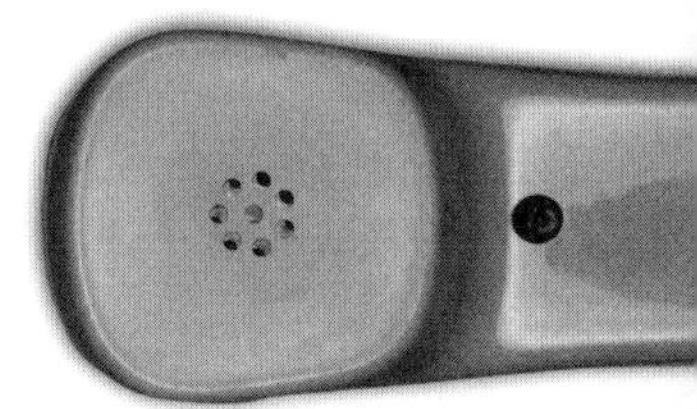

# Decision making

MUCH HAS BEEN WRITTEN ABOUT the process by which decision makers make decisions. It is beyond the scope of this book (and this author) to pinpoint the best. Instead, this chapter offers three perspectives that may help in identifying those factors most important to a given executive and to respond to these priorities successfully.

## FIVE STYLES

### Recognize and respond.

*In their 2007 "Harvard Business Review" article, Gary A. Williams and Robert B. Miller contend that business decision-making styles fall into five categories and that a targeted persuasive strategy is appropriate for each.*

## ADOLESCENTS

### Remember that some people never grow up.

Another perspective, often quoted by colleges and university career centers, comes from the work of L. B. Dinkage, describing the decision-making styles of adolescents. These styles are offered here in the belief that growing older does not necessarily change the way a person makes decisions.

Table 1

| Style | Decision-Maker's Characteristics | Persuader's Strategy | Examples |
|---|---|---|---|
| Charismatic | Easily enthralled, but bases final decisions on balanced information; emphasizes bottom line results | Focus on results; make straightforward arguments; stress proposal's benefits with visual aids; use buzzwords like *proven*, *actions*, *easy*, *clear* | Lee Iacocca, Herb Kelleher |
| Thinker | Toughest to persuade; cerebral; logical; risk averse; needs extensive detail | Present market research, customer surveys, case studies, cost/benefit analyses; use buzzwords like *quality*, *numbers*, *expert*, *proof* | Michael Dell, Bill Gates |
| Skeptic | Challenges every data point; decides based on gut feelings | Establish credibility with endorsements from someone the CEO trusts; use buzzwords like *grasp*, *power*, *suspect*, *trust* | Larry Ellison, Tom Siebel |

(Continued on next page)

**Table 1** (continued)

| | | | |
|---|---|---|---|
| Follower | Relies on own or other's past decisions to make current choices; late adopter | Use testimonials to prove low risk; present innovative, yet proven solutions; use buzzwords like *expertise*, *similar to*, *innovate*, *previous* | Peter Coors, Carly Fiorina |
| | | | |
| Controller | Unemotional; analytical; abhors uncertainty; only implements own ideas | Present highly structured arguments; make listener "own" the idea; avoid aggressive advocacy; use buzzwords like *fact*, *reason*, *power*, *just do it* | Ross Perot, Martha Stewart |

1. *Impulsive*—You are likely to have taken the first, most convenient option or alternative that was presented without much, or any, thought of the outcome.
2. *Fatalistic*—You are likely to have left the decision open to fate. You are likely to have waited to see what happened, feeling perhaps that something would occur that would indicate the right direction, or that you would be somehow guided to the right path.
3. *Delaying*—You are likely to have responded by not worrying too much about the decision and delayed making one until you really had to decide.
4. *Compliant*—You are likely to have been influenced by the plans of others and molded your own decisions in line with this majority view. This was done to keep the

peace or to do what you thought was best for the majority.

5. *Agonizing*—It was likely that you spent excessive time gathering a lot of information—then got swamped by it! You gathered so much data that you were overwhelmed by the seemingly endless options, which put you back to square one!

6. *Planning*—You tended to gather the information needed, analyzed it as best you could, and then used your instincts to make the final choice.

7. *Intuitive*—You made decisions based primarily on what you felt; you used your intuition as the main source of your responses to the decisions and problems.

8. *Paralytic*—You knew you just had to make a decision; you wanted to make a decision, but you were frozen into immobility because you were worried about the consequences. You knew you had to face up to the responsibility and the decision, but it worried you rigid (and perhaps still does!).

9. *Escapist*—You tended to escape to a fantasy or semi–fantasy world when faced with hard decisions in the past. You tended to imagine possible futures and decisions that were beyond your short-term (or even long-term) abilities. Alternatively, you might have come up with a socially acceptable answer, but one that was not really right for you.

10. *Play-safe*—You tended to make the decision based on the lowest risk, or the safest bet, for you at the time. You chose the option that gave you the least hassle, even when you felt it wasn't quite right.

11. *Deviant*—You were inclined to be a bit of a rebel when it came to some past decision. If someone suggested one

direction, you were likely to choose the other. You didn't want to appear as if you agreed with others; you wanted to be, or wanted to appear to be, more independent minded, even if you later regretted the decision made.

(Source: Dinklage, L. B. 1968. *Decision strategies of adolescents*, doctoral dissertation, Harvard University, Cambridge, MA).

## WHO TO AVOID

### Hang up and move on.

Finally, there are certain types of decision makers that are best avoided. They either lack authority or make the selling process so difficult that calling on them is not worth the effort.

*Advice seekers*—Generally, it's a good sign when decision makers ask for your advice in solving a business problem. However, in some cases, the prospect is just fishing for information and has no intention of buying.

*Bargainers*—These prospects specialize in whittling down your offering, especially your price. They'll ask what something costs before they're even sure what it does. They demean your product's features, belittle its benefits, and then offer to buy it for 70 percent off.

*Braggarts*—Some people spend all their time telling you how great they are and how many wonderful things they've done for their company. They have no interest in your product because they didn't invent the product themselves.

*Complainers*—These people monopolize your time with complaints about something: their jobs, their bosses, their companies, the state of the world. Don't try to comfort them with your solution. They're not really interested.

*Cowards*—These prospects can't seem to say "no" even though they never have any intent on buying. Initially, they sound interested and may even arrange meetings and conference calls. But after a flurry of enthusiasm, they never answer the phone again.

*Dreamers*—Like many of us, some decision makers have wants that far exceed their means. These people appreciate the quality of your offering and visualize themselves using it. They're excited about what it could mean to their success and spend considerable amounts of time soaking in the details and your sales pitch. In the end, they're small timers who want to play in the big leagues but simply cannot afford it.

*Efficiency experts*—This type of decision maker insists that every conceivable detail be discussed, written, checked, and double-checked. Failure to do so will void the sale. Too often, this person concludes that nothing is good enough and buys nothing.

*Family members*—More and more young adults are working for their parents. However, the parents inevitably have sole buying authority. If you sense that the person is a child of the decision maker, ask that person whether he/she can make a final decision. In dealing with spouses, remember that, in most cases, the pair must agree on major buying decisions. If you can't sell both of them, write it off.

*Fame seekers*—These leaders are only interested in changes that sound good in newspapers and trade journals. If you're selling cutting-edge technology, that's good. If you're selling nuts-and-bolts improvements, don't expect much traction from this kind of decision maker.

*Hanger-on-ers*—These VIPs stretch the sales process from weeks to months to years. In the end, they don't buy anything. They give you a call-back date but don't answer the phone when you call. When you do reach them, they give you another date . . . again and again until you get worn out chasing your tail.

*Idiots*—Some decision makers are simply stupid, at least as far as understanding your product. No matter how you try to explain, these folks can't (or won't) grasp what you're saying. Hang up ASAP.

*Impulse buyers*—Some decision makers act quickly. In most cases, this is an ideal situation. However, before celebrating, ensure that the VIP has the authority and budget to execute the purchase. This kind of person is also prone to buyer's remorse, with a tendency to undecide as quickly as he decides.

*Jerks*—Some decision makers are jerks (boorish, arrogant, insulting human beings who seem to take pleasure in torturing unsuspecting salespeople). Hang up before you scream. The aggravation of this person's business far outweighs any benefits you might derive.

*Job applicants*—Occasionally, you'll receive a hit on your website from a legitimate-sounding person at a legitimate business only to discover that he/she is actually looking for a job with your company. Usually, the tell-tale sign is that the person's e-mail address is generic and not specific to the company.

*Leavers*—These folks are actually planning to leave their jobs soon. When you call, you discover that, soon, they'll be taking a new job, retiring, or laid off. No thanks! No help.

*Pseudo executives*—These are decision makers who are "playing" business. They seem more interested in forms, job titles, and procedural correctness than in bottom-line facts. These people are unlikely to buy since new products rarely fit into their artificial worlds.

*Researchers*—Some people are constantly gathering information about this or that. They search the Internet day after day downloading product descriptions and white papers just for curiosity. Maybe they're daydreaming. Maybe they're thinking about creating a competing product. But they're never actually planning on buying anything.

*Rule followers*—These decision makers are more interested in process than in outcome. They refuse to commit themselves to anything other than referring your information to someone else. After a while, it's apparent that most of these folks aren't decision makers at all. They either lack authority or they're too afraid to use it. Either way, they're useless.

*Snobs*—These folks pride themselves on being in the "in crowd" or at least near it. They want to know whether you have any prestigious customers or know any famous people. If you have A-list references, play them. If not, don't expect to get very far with these folks.

*Spies*—Occasionally, a spy will appear on the radar screen, someone from a competing company who's trying to gather product or pricing details to use against you. Most often these sleazes show up on your website, registered under a generic-sounding name, a company name with initials only, a bogus phone number, and an e-mail address that ends in Yahoo, Hotmail, or something similar.

*Storytellers*—Some decision makers like to talk about themselves for extended periods. Some of these never get down to business.

*Survivors*—These people deserve sympathy, but won't be buying anything anytime soon. They've just survived a major layoff, an industry downturn, or some other disaster affecting the organization. They're afraid and in shock. Offer brief consolation . . . and move on.

*Team captains*—These decision makers must confer with a variety of co-workers before buying anything. Typically, this involves a series of team meetings, held over several months, generally reaching no conclusions. Don't waste too much time on this type of VIP.

*Visionaries*—These leaders have magnificent visions for the future that fit perfectly with what you're selling. Unfortunately, they rarely buy. They're thinking so far out into the future that countless details must be settled before your offering can be evaluated. In the end, they change their plans—dropping your solution from the mix—or move on to another job and another vision.

# CHAPTER SIXTEEN

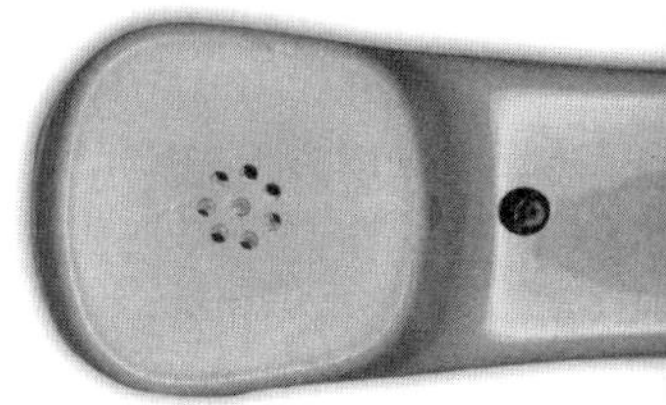

# Names

ONE OF THE MOST CRITICAL and most difficult aspects of telemarketing is identifying decision makers by name. This chapter offers proven suggestions for determining the right people to call.

## IN-HOUSE INFORMATION

### Check your records.

The first step in identifying contacts by name is to use the information you already have in hand. If you have a master database of sales prospects, build on it. Do you have other sales leads on index cards or paper forms that haven't been entered into the database? Do individual sales reps have their own databases that could be integrated into the master list? If your organization belongs to an association of prospective buyers, do you have, or can you get, a membership list? Do you have any partners who could supply contact names?

## COMPANY WEBSITE

### Search their site.

Let's say that you want to find the name of the chief information officer (CIO) at Broadview Manufacturing Corporation. The first step is to look at the company's website (if they have one). If you don't know the Web address (URL) for the company, go to www.Google.com, type "Broadview Manufacturing" in quotations, and press search. The first listing should be the company's site. (Note: By placing the name is quotes, you're telling Google that you're only interested in Internet pages that have these two words together. Without the quotes, you might get an entry that contained the word *Broadview* but did not concern this particular company.)

If the company has a website, look for the CIO's name in several places:

Under the "About Us" page, see if there's a listing of officers or administration leaders. The CIO's name may appear there.

Under the "News" section, look for press releases that concern computer technology or for stories/photos showing company employees. The CIO may be listed.

## INTERNET SEARCH

### Google it.

Google is the best invention since sliced bread! For the first time in history, you can thoroughly research any topic on the Internet from the convenience of your own PC. I'd be lost without it.

While most people understand the basics of using Google, you can visit http://www.google.com/help/basics.html for an overview.

I use Google to identify decision makers by title. For example, if I'm trying to identify the CIO, I search on company name, city, and the letters "CIO." Often, articles will appear quoting the CIO by name. Presto! (This kind of search also yields lots of references to the AFL-CIO or other CIO references that have nothing to do with the CIO. No problem. Just scan past those results to the good stuff.)

If you know the decision maker's name, Google is also invaluable in gathering additional details about the person. Typically, the larger the organization, the more likely it is that a major player will have at least one Internet reference. You may find the person's name listed within the company's website, on a list of association members or conference attendees, or quoted in an industry news article. Reading those quotes can help you understand the VIP's priorities and business philosophy. Sometimes you'll discover that the organization has already purchased a product similar to yours or that the decision maker doesn't believe in the technology you're selling. Sometimes you'll find that the person is actually looking for a product exactly like yours—oh, happy day!

Sometimes in the process of researching a decision maker, I come across the name of that person's second-in-command. For example, an article might quote the top guy but make reference in later paragraphs to the assistant director who is actually implementing whatever is being discussed. While reaching C-level (top-tier) leaders is best, reaching B-level is often more realistic and, initially, more productive.

Finally, searching the Internet for a particular topic can yield important clues. For example, when I sold software that enables doctors to access patient data on PDAs, I searched Google using the name of the hospital plus entries such as "PDA" and "mobile technology." Sometimes, I learned that the hospital had already deployed a competing solution. Sometimes, I learned that the institution had a well-funded project to purchase this technology.

## LOCAL PUBLICATIONS

### Check the news stand.

For contact names in your local area, read the business section of your local newspaper and search through any vertical marketing publications published locally. For example, in my community, there are magazines for small business owners, upscale homeowners, apartment renters, car buyers, parents, senior citizens, spiritualists, and naturalists. Look at the articles, news announcements, and advertising. The local chamber of commerce membership directory is also an excellent way to identify business and institutional executives.

## LIST BROKERS

### Buy the information.

Data gained from list brokers can be valuable in two ways: (1) by providing a database of all companies you want to target, so that you can be sure that you haven't missed anybody, and (2) by providing high-level, specialized contact names. For example, if you're looking for decision makers in a hospital setting, you can purchase a database from the American Hospital Association. For accurate up-to-date lists of professionals such as lawyers, engineers, accountants, and architects, go to the professional association representing each group.

You can find a printed directory of national associations at your local library or at one of these websites:

http://www.asaecenter.org/Directories/AssociationSearch.cfm

http://www.marketingsource.com/associations/

A directory of nonprofit associations can be found at http://www.ncna.org/.

Specialized business publications are also a good source of contact names. For example, if you're targeting safety officials at manufacturing facilities, you can contact *Facility Safety Management* magazine about getting a subscriber list. http://www.facilitysafetymgt.com/

To search for publications serving your target audience, go to http://www.mediafinder.com/demo/indexe.cfm.

## ASKING

### Charm to disarm.

When in doubt, ask the receptionist, who can be very helpful if approached in a pleasant, respectful manner.

One strategy is to ask for the decision maker by title:

*Who is the regional manager of your company?*

As a rule, this is a bad idea, since the receptionist is the frontline gatekeeper, trained to protect VIPs from uninvited callers like you. Even so, I'm surprised how often receptionists will offer a contact name when approached in a nice way.

Another approach is to ask for the receptionist's help:

Receptionist: *Acme Controls. How can I help you?*

You: *Yes. This is Alex Brown. How are you today?*

Receptionist: *Fine. How can I help you?*

You: *I just need some information, please. I'm trying to reach the person who manages your computer system. Who would that be?*

If you don't get the decision maker's name, you may be automatically transferred to his phone. If the VIP answers, introduce yourself and ask for the name. If you get voice mail instead, listen to the name announcement during the voice-mail prompt. With a little luck, you'll hear the direct extension, too.

*Hello. This is Bob Sutterwhite at Extension 455.*
*Please leave me a message at the tone.*

If you're not transferred directly to the decision maker's phone, you may be connected to a general department number or to the VIP's administrative assistant. In this case, ask the person who answers whether he/she is the right person to speak with about your topic and, if not, ask who would be the right person. Keep asking the same question in a polite, innocent manner, accepting transfer after transfer, until you reach the right person.

# PART 5

# GOALS & PRIORITIES

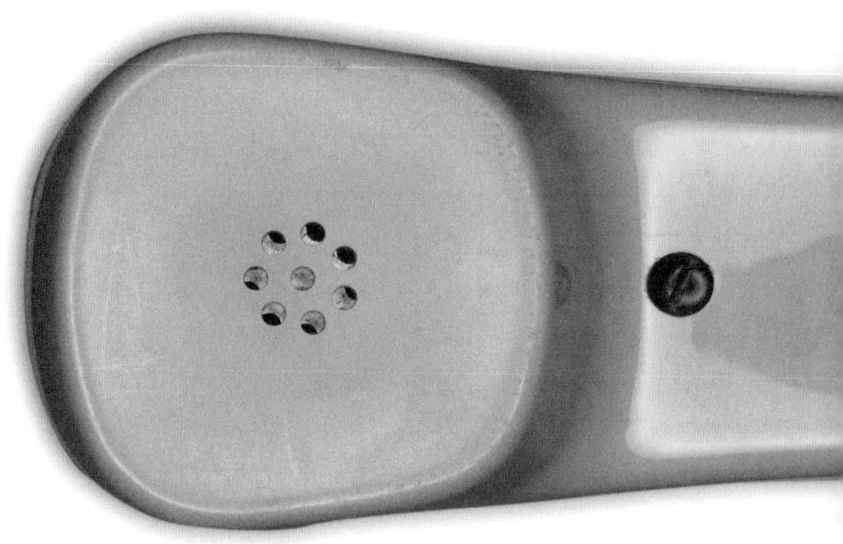

# CHAPTER SEVENTEEN

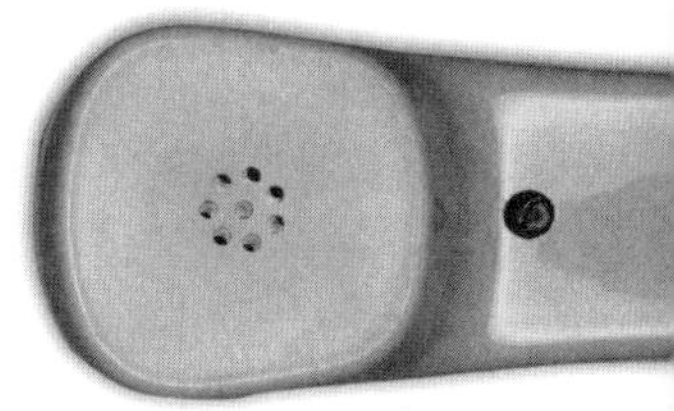

# Set a course

AS DISCUSSED EARLIER, TELEMARKETING WITHOUT a clear direction is likely to result in lots of calls and few accomplishments. Every campaign needs measurable objectives that provide focus and accountability to the effort.

## THE BALANCE

### Be challenging yet realistic.

An effective goal has two parts: (1) the objective to be accomplished, and (2) the period of time in which the objective is to be accomplished. For example, a typical goal might be to make ten dials per hour. This is measurable and time phased.

Goals should also be challenging, yet realistic. Maybe you decide to make twenty dials per hour. That's certainly challenging, but is it realistic considering other aspects of the telemarketer's job, such as record keeping, product education, and company meetings? Some managers intentionally set unrealistic goals with the thought that expecting more will generate greater results. This kind of manager typically believes that human beings are essentially lazy and will only do what they're forced to do. Faced with his workers' failure to meet these unrealistic goals, this manager uses criticism and threats to prod production. Sooner than later, the better telemarketers quit, and a new batch is hired to fill the treadmill.

Besides the fact that it's cruel to punish employees for failing to do the impossible, it's also counterproductive. How are these belittled, unappreciated callers likely to sound on the phone? Will they be energetic and cheerful? Are they likely to promote the company's products in a positive manner? The answer, of course, is NO!

What short-sighted taskmasters fail to understand is that the number of people who may buy any given product is limited. The more specialized the product, the more limited are the potential buyers. Even when there are many thousands of potential buyers, the number of prospects within that target group with the highest potential to buy is relatively small.

Realizing this limitation, every phone call is important. Having unhappy, overstressed telemarketers calling your most precious prospects not only reduces short-term sales, but may alienate these prospects from ever buying in the future. Companies who are oblivious to this reality lose out today and tomorrow.

The other reality is that the number of reliable employees who are willing and able to make telemarketing calls is also limited, at least in America. Using and abusing these folks will eventually lead to empty phones calling no one.

The point is that a company's goals should be challenging, but must also be realistic in order to service a company's target audience and maintain a high quality workforce.

If you are setting your own goals, be realistic with yourself. Setting goals too high will doom you to failure and reduce your ability and willingness to make calls hour after hour, day after day. Setting goals too low is just a way to avoid the hard work that successful telemarketing requires.

As discussed below, there are two types of goals:

Process goals: the specific actions you intend to take

Outcome goals: the specific results you expect from these actions

## PROCESS GOALS

### Decide how many and how soon.

*Number of dials*—The most basic type of process goal concerns the number of people to be called within a unit of time. Generally referred to as the number of *dials*, outbound calls actually involve six distinct steps:

1. Dialing the number
2. Waiting as the phone rings
3. Maneuvering past a receptionist or voice-mail system to reach the person's direct number
4. Speaking with the person or leaving a message
5. Sending follow-up information
6. Recording the transaction in your internal records

Dialing, waiting, and recording (steps 1, 2 and 6) can be accomplished quickly. The time it takes maneuvering, communicating with the decision maker, and sending follow-up information (steps 3, 4, and 5) can vary greatly depending on the situation. You can get lost in some voice-mail systems or be transferred from person to person without actually reaching your intended contact. Leaving a message with an individual takes longer than leaving a voice mail. And of course, if you're lucky enough to actually reach the contact on the phone, your conversation time can vary from twenty seconds to twenty minutes. Sending follow-up literature can be done quickly by e-mail, but will require additional time if individualized and/or mailed in printed form. As a result, the average dials per hour, for example, may be difficult to predict.

As a general guideline, one B2B telemarketer can make approximately seventy-five energetic dials in an eight-hour period performing all six steps outlined below. This estimate reflects time spent away from the phone for coffee and restroom breaks, staff meetings, and product training.

A legitimate issue for callers and their managers regards how much time should be spent researching an account before calling into it. For example, in making calls to high-level decision makers in large organizations who are not already identified by name, I may spend three hours in research for every thirty minutes I actually spend on the phone. In calling a list of existing customers to promote renewal of a $100 educational newsletter, I devote 100 percent of my time to dialing.

I'm reminded of a story about Thomas Edison, who had helped Henry Ford design his first Model-T factory. One day, a large machine in the factory stopped working, and Ford sent for Edison, who repaired the machine in five minutes. A few days later, Ford received a bill for $5,000. "That's outrageous!" Ford wrote back to Edison. "You only worked for five minutes." "True," Edison replied, "and worth every penny!"

In telemarketing, results are king! If you only make one call a day and that call results in a big-ticket sale, you're a hero. If you make one hundred calls a day and sell nothing, you may be a hard worker; but you're still a failure when judged by the bottom line. It's that simple. Edison only needed five minutes to make $5,000 because he knew exactly what to do. The more you know, the better you'll perform.

*Reached*—The second major process goal concerns the number of people you actually reach, usually measured as a percentage of those called.

Generally, this percentage is dependent upon three variables: (1) the type of position held by the decision maker within the organization; (2) the size of the organization, usually measured by its number of employees; and (3) whether the organization is a public institution, such as a unit of government or school, or a for-profit business. Using these variables, you can predict that higher-level leaders are harder to reach than lower-level; those in larger enterprises are harder to reach than those in smaller; and those in for-profit companies are harder to reach than those in public organizations.

The following chart illustrates these conclusions.

**Table 2**

| Position | Organization | Employees | Reach % | Per 1000 |
|---|---|---|---|---|
| CEO | Private | 1-10 | 15.00% | 150 |
| | | 11-50 | 5.00% | 50 |
| | | 51-250 | 1.00% | 10 |
| | | 251-999 | 0.50% | 5 |
| | | 1000+ | 0.05% | > 1 |
| | Govt/Public | 1-10 | 20.00% | 200 |
| | | 11-50 | 7.50% | 75 |
| | | 51-250 | 3.25% | 33 |
| | | 251-999 | 0.80% | 8 |
| | | 1000+ | 0.10% | 1 |

(Continued on next page)

Table 2 (continued)

| Position | Organization | Employees | Reach % | Per 1000 |
|---|---|---|---|---|
| COO/CFO/ | Private | 1-10 | 20.00% | 200 |
| | | 11-50 | 10.00% | 100 |
| | | 51-250 | 5.00% | 50 |
| | | 251-999 | 1.00% | 10 |
| | | 1000+ | 0.50% | 5 |
| | Govt/Public | 1-10 | 25.00% | 250 |
| | | 11-50 | 12.50% | 125 |
| | | 51-250 | 6.25% | 63 |
| | | 251-999 | 3.12% | 32 |
| | | 1000+ | 0.75% | 8 |
| | | | | |
| 2nd Level Managers | Private | 1-10 | 25.00% | 250 |
| | | 11-50 | 15.00% | 150 |
| | | 51-250 | 10.00% | 100 |
| | | 251-999 | 5.00% | 50 |
| | | 1000+ | 1.00% | 10 |
| | Govt/Public | 1-10 | 30.00% | 300 |
| | | 11-50 | 20.00% | 200 |
| | | 51-250 | 10.00% | 100 |
| | | 251-999 | 5.00% | 50 |
| | | 1000+ | 2.00% | 20 |

## OUTCOME GOALS

### Excel on the bottom line.

If you make a thousand calls a day, reach 90 percent of the people you call, and still don't sell anything, what good is it? Ultimately, your effort must lead to results, or you're out of business.

*Direct selling*—If you're trying to sell products directly by phone, you can easily measure the number of sales you've accomplished in a given period of time. You may set a goal of selling a given number of units or a sales amount. You may want to establish a goal of selling to a certain percentage of people you call or a certain percentage of those you reach.

Ultimately, you can divide the amount you earn by the amount of time you spent calling to determine an hourly rate of return. For example, I once owned a business that had a few great days and lots of bad ones. One day, I divided all the money I had made by all the hours I had worked and discovered that I was earning less than $3.00 an hour. I could have made twice as much money by working at McDonalds—and gotten free food! Eventually, I closed that enterprise and starting fishing elsewhere.

*Lead generation*—If your intent is to generate sales leads rather than close sales by phone, setting measurable outcome goals becomes more difficult. Instead of dollars and cents, results are determined by the number of people interested in your product and their degree of interest.

So how do you know whether a person is interested in what you're selling? Occasionally, you know because the prospect says so directly. "Yes! I'm interested. That sounds good! Wow! That's a great product! When can you deliver it? This is exactly what I've been looking for!" When you hear any of these words, rejoice! You've hit the jackpot.

A prospect will also make it abundantly clear when he/she is definitely *not* interested: "Forget it! Get out of here! No way! Are you kidding?!? Don't call me again!" In these cases, "No!" means "No!"

But what about everybody else? I determine the degree of a prospect's interest based on what that person is willing to do next. The categories below are arranged from highest to lowest interest:

Table 3

| Interest Level | Definition |
|---|---|
| 1 | Wants to meet with an outside sales rep |
| 2 | Wants to talk with an outside rep by phone to discuss pricing, technical details, etc. |
| 3 | Wants to participate in an online product demonstration |
| 4 | Wants a call back on a specific date within the next 30 days |
| 5 | Wants a call back within the next "couple of months" without setting a specific phone appointment |
| 6 | Wants a call back in six months |
| 7 | Wants a call back next year |

The term *lead* has different meanings to different people. I consider a lead to be a prospect that is so interested in the product that an outside sales rep should follow-up with him/her. Using the chart above, I would consider anyone at a level 1 or 2 to be a lead and would transition that person to an outside rep for follow-up.

Back to the question of outcome goals in regards to lead generation.... This can be as simple or as complicated as you want to make it.

My general rule of thumb is that at least 5 percent of the people I call should express interest in what I'm selling. (Using the chart above, I would define "interested" as those at levels 1–4.) If the interest level falls below that level, I consider there to be a selling problem—I'm calling the wrong people, selling the wrong product, charging the wrong price, calling at the wrong time, and/or saying the wrong things.

## IN THE END

### Keep your eye on the big picture.

In the end, I have five goals that I try to accomplish in every telemarketing situation:

1. Convince the interested to buy.
2. Persuade the undecided to be interested.
3. Eliminate the ones who will never buy.
4. Leave a favorable impression about the company with everyone.
5. Help the people I call.

# CHAPTER EIGHTEEN

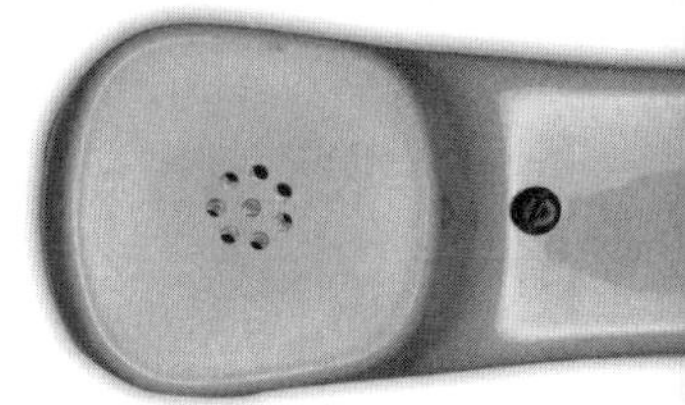

## Eat dessert first

REMEMBER WHEN YOUR MOTHER SAID that you couldn't eat your dessert until you finished your spinach? Selling is just the opposite. You get to eat every hot fudge sundae you can find before you have to start on the veggies.

In sales lingo, it's called "picking the low-hanging fruit." Ben Franklin called it "a bird in the hand." I call it doing the easy thing first. Simply, your first call of the day should be to the sales prospect most likely to buy today; the second one, to the next most likely; and so forth.

Like our mothers, not everybody agrees with the "fun first" approach. Once I worked for a health newsletter publisher selling subscription renewals to hospitals and medical clinics. Based on my experience during my first six months at the company and my analysis of renewal statistics gathered over several years prior, I determined that a certain group of prospects was twice as likely to renew than other customers. Like the alchemist who was sure he had uncovered the secret of turning lead into gold, I rushed to the owner with my discovery. He was not pleased.

"I want you to call everybody," he snorted, "not just the good prospects." After reassuring him that I did plan to call everyone on my list, I suggested that the most lucrative approach would be to call the best prospects first.

He was even less pleased, telling me in no uncertain terms that he hadn't hired me to make the easy sales, but the hard ones. Besides, he said, "It's more of a motivator if you don't know which leads are better than others. That way, you'll try harder to close everybody."

At this point, I realized that he was probably thinking of that rat experiment in psychology class where the rat pushes a pedal to get a food pellet. When the rewards are given on a random basis, the rat pushes the petal continuously looking for its unpredictable reward.

However, the difference between a rat and a person—among other things—is that a rat can't visualize other alternatives. While it may perform instinctually again and again until exhaustion, a human being will look for a better way, a more efficient way, a more controllable way to gain rewards. It's called invention.

The epilogue to this story is that, after several heated debates with my boss about the benefits of prioritizing, he prioritized my butt out the door. I was right, but I was unemployed.

## RANKING SYSTEMS

### Find out who's on first.

Identifying telemarketing priorities can be as simple or as complicated as you want to make it. If you're calling a handful of companies (one hundred or fewer), you can highlight the best ones on a piece of paper. However, if you're calling thousands, you need an automated system.

For example, when working for a software company selling to hospitals, I developed a numerical rating system based on the characteristics of each hospital and the degree of interest expressed by its leaders.

First, I researched the company's existing customers and determined that the majority of buyers had these characteristics:

1. 250–500 beds (licensed size)
2. Located in an urban area instead of a rural one
3. Located in an area with higher-than-average population growth
4. Located in a county with five or less competitors

Then for each variable, I assigned a value for each characteristic:

Bed size

- 250–500 beds = 10 points
- 100–249 beds or with 500 beds or more = 5 points
- Fewer than 100 beds = 1 point

Urban area

- Yes = 10 points
- No = 1 point

Population growth

- Above average = 10 points
- Average = 5 points
- Below average = 1 point

Competitors

- 5 or less = 10 points
- 6–10 = 5 points

By using this weighted point system, I determined a "Characteristics Score" for each noncustomer hospital. For example, a hospital that had the same characteristics as our customers would have a Characteristics Score of 40.

I then calculated an "Interest Score" for each account by multiplying (1) the degree of interest in the product by (2) the level of authority of the person expressing the interest.

(1) The degree of interest was calculated as follows:
  20 points = Interested now (will buy within 6 months)
  15 points = Interested later (will buy within 7–12 months)
  10 points = Unable to reach
  5 points = Not interested due to budget/low priority
  1 point = Not interested; bought a competing product
  0 points = Closed/out of business

(2) Authority values were as follows:
  10 points = C level (CIO, CEO, chief of staff)
  5 points = B level (computer manager, assistant to CEO, etc.)
  1 point = A level (analyst, administrative assistant, etc.)

The overall priority rating of each account was calculated by adding the Characteristics Score to the Interest Score.

In this way, I was able to numerically rank all hospitals from the most likely to buy to the least likely.

## CAUTION

### Just do it!

A final word of caution: I had a college roommate who spent so much time organizing his homework that he never had time to do it. As a successful telemarketer, you need to balance the time you spend researching, organizing, and prioritizing prospects with the time you spend actually calling on them. Adequate preparation is essential. Excessive preparation can be an excuse not to pick up the phone.

# PART 6

# MASTER DATABASE

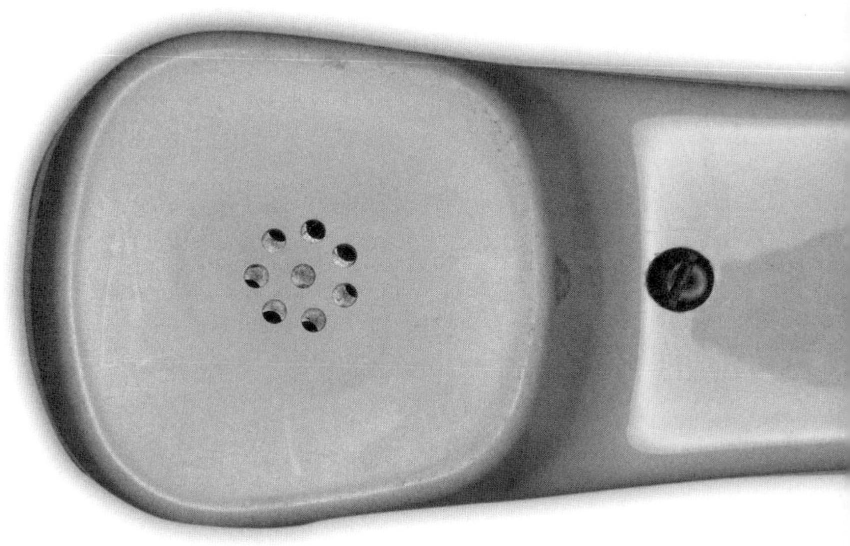

# CHAPTER NINETEEN

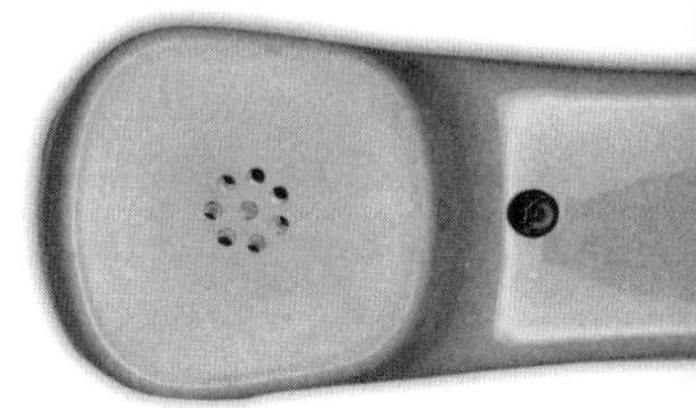

# Compiling data

A COMPLETE AND ACCURATE MASTER database of the most important sales prospects is one of the most valuable assets any business can possess. And yet, few companies have one.

Never in my twenty-five plus years of providing telemarketing services as an employee or contractor have I ever found a consolidated master database when I began work. Usually, the records were both electronic and on paper. The computer files were in different formats and in different locations. Gathered from a myriad of sources such as trade shows, Web inquiries, cold calling, and outside lists, the data included leads of every stage in the sales process, mixing customer names with prospects and good leads with bad.

When the information was in one electronic file, duplicate records, incomplete records, and useless records abounded. The state of the data reflected the typical sales mentality—sell as much as you can as fast as you can—and leave the residue behind you. Why waste time with updating files when there are places to go and people to see?

If you have an endless stream of customers beating your door down or an infinite number of great prospects, you don't need to consolidate and organize prospect data. You just need help carrying money to the bank. (Any jobs open at your place?)

But if your business is like most, you still need new customers. The number of top-quality prospects is limited, and you only have so much time to chase them. Get organized! Consolidate all your data into one source with a consistent format, clean it up, and keep it updated.

## CLEAN-UP

### Find the weirdos.

Old lists and new unused lists typically require a certain degree of clean-up. For example, correct misspellings, partial phone numbers, addresses without states or zip codes, and first names without last names and vice versa. For a professional look in generating automated letters and e-mails, reformat the data into lower- and uppercase rather than having some records completely in uppercase.

This process ultimately requires a record-by-record examination of the data. Learn to scan records quickly, like speed reading, looking for letters and numbers that are out of place relative to the correct data. For example, if you are looking down a long list of zip codes, you will recognize the ones without five digits.

## DE-DUPING

### Don't blow it.

Remove duplicate records. While there may be more automated strategies, I remove duplicate records by sorting the data in various ways and eyeballing it one record at a time. Whether the data is in an Excel file or in another format, you can sort by three variables at once. Start by sorting on

(1) last name, (2) first name, and then (3) company. After you've de-duped in this way, sort by phone number and then by e-mail address.

One of the most embarrassing moments in telemarketing occurs when you accidentally call someone twice. You've just had an honest productive conversation, establishing your credibility and generating interest in your product. All is well. Then thirty minutes later, without recognizing the duplicate name, you call the same person again and deliver your standard introductory line only to hear the decision maker say, "Didn't we just talk a few minutes ago?"

Suddenly and irrevocably, the prospect that felt so special a few minutes ago feels cheap and unimportant. Like the girl who knows a guy is dating other people, she can handle it as long as he doesn't put it in her face. If you've done a good job the first time, the person you're calling has made an individual connection with you that feels unique. Don't blow it with sloppy record keeping.

> "I never tell a one client that I cannot attend his sales convention because I have a previous engagement with another client.
> Successful polygamy depends upon pretending to each spouse that she is the only pebble on your beach."
>
> —David Ogilvy

## REFORMATTING

### Make it consistent.

*Names*—Contact names in different files are often formatted differently. One file may have the first and last name in the same field. Another may have the first name in a field separate from the last. Some files may have salutation terms (Mr.,

Dr., Ms.) and family extensions (Jr., III), while others may not.

Based on the software you use for the master database, you will need to make the names consistent, keeping the full name in one field or the first and last names in separate fields. (My advice is to eliminate family extensions and to include only the salutation Dr. either preceding the full name or the first name, depending on your format.)

Sounds like a good idea, except who wants to reenter thousands of names to make them consistent? No problem. There's a relatively simple way to reformat the data using Excel.

Let's start with records that have the full name in one field and need to be converted into two fields, one for the first name and the other for the last name.

- Create an Excel spreadsheet for the file you want to change. You may already have the data in that format. If not, most database programs will allow you to easily export the data into an Excel file.
- Open Microsoft Word. Type a few letters then save the file in a plain text format. I usually name the file "Fix.txt" and place it on my desktop for easy access.
- Highlight the name column in the Excel file and copy it.
- Paste the data into the text file. Manually delete any extraneous data that is not the first name or last name (prefixes such as Mr. or Ms., middle initials, period marks, etc.). Save and close.
- Open the text file in Word.
  (1) Go to Edit/Select all to highlight all the data.
  (2) Go to Edit/Replace.
  (3) Complete the "Find what" field by going to More/ Special/ and select White Space.

(4) Type a comma in the "Replace with" field.
(5) Click "Replace all."
(6) A comma will appear between the first and last name.
(7) Save. (It will remain a text file.)

- Open Excel.
- Open the text file.
- Select "delimited."
- On the next screen, uncheck "tab" delimited, and check "comma" delimited. Press OK.

  The first names will now appear in column one, and the last name in column two. Correct any data that is misaligned. Label each column.
- Save as an Excel file. I usually name this "Add.xls" and save it to the desktop.
- Highlight the two columns. Copy.
- Open your original Excel file; that is, the one in which the name is all in one column.
  (1) Make sure that each column in this file is labeled.
  (2) Insert two empty columns to the right of the name column.
  (3) Paste the data from Add.xls into these two columns. Now the column with the full name should be next to the columns with the first and last name separated. Make sure that these align correctly.
  (4) Delete the column with both names together.
  (5) Save.

Yes, this process sounds complicated. But it only takes about fifteen minutes compared to hours for reentering the data.

Now, let's examine the opposite problem with contact names. You want the first and last name to be in one field, but you have a database in which these names are in separate fields.

In this case, process the records in a method similar to that outlined previously. To summarize the steps:

- Copy the first and last name columns out of an Excel spreadsheet.
- Paste them into a text file. Save. Close.
- Open the text file with Word. You'll see the names with two white spaces between the first and last names. To delete the extra white space,
  (1) go to Find/Replace and select white space. Then put the symbol twice in the find column.
  (2) In the replace column put only one white space symbol.
  (3) Select replace all.
  (4) Save
- Open Excel. Open the text file. Click "Finish." You should see all the names combined, all in column one, each on a separate row. Save as an Excel file. "Add.xls" will be okay as a name.
- Copy the column and insert into the original Excel file.

*Job titles*—Official job titles can also vary widely. There are managers, directors, executives, chiefs, administrators, supervisors, partners, heads, and leads. How do you compare apples and oranges? Is the chief technical officer the same as a chief information officer? Is an assistant manager the same as assistant to the manager? If consistently classifying by duty or rank is important to you, you'll want to make those adjustments in your master database.

*Company*—Make the company name consistent. For example, if you have one contact person at Acme International and another at Acme, Inc., it's important to determine whether these people work for the same place by comparing addresses and telephone numbers of the companies. If they are the same, pick the correct company spelling and label both records in the same manner. Otherwise, you'll trip over yourself calling two VIPs from the same place without knowing it.

*Addresses*—If you're planning to mail any information via the post office, you'll need the correct mailing address. If you're planning to send packages via UPS or FedEx, you'll need the correct street address. Multiple records for the company may have one and not the other. If you have both, but can only record one, pick the street address. It works for all types of deliveries.

*Phone*—The company will have a main number, while a specific contact may have a different direct number. Maintain both if possible. If you only have room for one in your database, retain the direct number.

*E-mail*—Again, when merging duplicate records, maintain the individual's e-mail address.

## MERGE/PURGE

### Get together.

So far, we've talked about making data consistent when two files have essentially the same fields. The next step is merging two files with different fields. While there are software programs that can merge/purge records, you can also accomplish this by using Excel. For example, here's how to merge Files A and B with the following fields:

Step 1: Make sure that both files are in an Excel format.

Step 2: Open File A (the file with the greater number of fields). Add any fields that are in File B that are not already in File A. (In this case, # Employees.) File A will then have nine columns. The first eight columns will have data. The last column, # Employees, will not. Save.

Table 4

| Fields | File A | File B |
|---|---|---|
| 1. First name | X | X |
| 2. Last name | X | X |
| 3. Job title | X | |
| 4. Company | X | X |
| 5. City | X | X |
| 6. State | X | X |
| 7. Phone | X | X |
| 8. E-mail | X | |
| 9. # Employees | | X |

Step 3: Open File B. Add any columns found in File A that are not already in File B. Arrange the columns in the same order as those in File A. Save.

Step 4: While in File B, change the color of the type from black to red. Save. Next highlight the first row of the spreadsheet. Next, pull the cursor down, one row after another, until all the data is highlighted. Finally, copy the highlighted data.

Step 5: Go back to File A. Move the cursor down the rows of the first column until you reach the last row in which data is found. Then highlight the row immediately following the last row of data. Next, paste the data from File B into File A. Save.

Step 6: Sort File A by last name and then by company.

Step 7: Review the data to find duplicate records. For example, if John Anderson at Harrington Corp. has a listing in both red and black, you know he appears on both lists. Manually enter any unique data from the red record into the black one. Then delete the red record. If a red record has no duplicate, do not change it.

Step 8: The end result of this process is a single database, without duplicate records. Change all the type to black (or any other color you prefer). Then save. Congrats! You have a master database.

## DO NOT CALL

### Respect their privacy.

The Telephone Consumer Protection Act (TCPA) established a Do-Not-Call Registry in 2003. Commercial telemarketers are not allowed to call consumers who have placed their phone numbers in this registry, subject to certain exceptions. The Federal Trade Commission (FTC) is responsible for enforcing these regulations and can impose significant fines on offenders.

Generally, B2B telemarketing calls are exempt from the Do-Not-Call Registry as explained in the following direct quote from the FTC website (http://www.ftc.gov/bcp/conline/pubs/buspubs/tsrcomp.shtm).

*Most phone calls between a telemarketer and a business are exempt from the Rule. But business-to-business calls to induce the retail sale of nondurable office or cleaning supplies are covered. Examples of nondurable office or cleaning supplies include paper, pencils, solvents, copying machine toner, and ink—in short, anything that, when used, is depleted, and must be replaced. Such goods as software, computer disks, copiers, computers, mops, and buckets are considered durable because they can be used again.*

*Although sellers and telemarketers involved in telemarketing sales to businesses of nondurable office or cleaning supplies must comply with the Rule's requirements and prohibitions, the Rule specifically exempts them from the recordkeeping requirements and from the National Do Not Call Registry provisions. These sellers and telemarketers do not have to create or keep any particular records, or purge numbers on the National Do Not Call Registry from their call lists to comply with the Rule.*

As most of us learned as kids, just because you can do something doesn't mean you should. Don't call people who don't want to be called. If a prospect indicates by phone or e-mail that he/she does not want to hear your charming voice over the phone lines, note this preference in your sales database and respect it.

## CHAPTER TWENTY

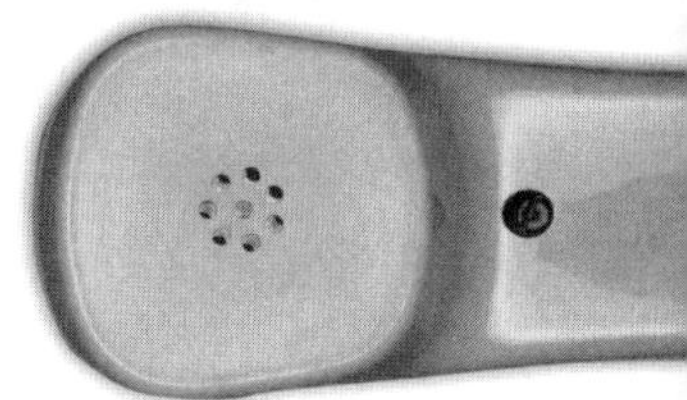

# Data management software

WHETHER YOU USE AN EXCEL spreadsheet or an expensive CRM (customer relationship management) program, you need to maintain your prospecting data in an electronic format. Paper forms, business cards, and sticky notes just won't cut it anymore. To be efficient, you must be able to quickly identify the demographics, status, and activity history of every company that you have called or plan to call. Certain data and functionality are essential.

## FIELDS

### Find a place for everything.

Essential: At a minimum, include these fields in your master database:

*First name*—Common name (Bill instead of William).

*Last name*

*Address*—Street address and suite number.

*City/State/Zip*

*Phone*—Area code, number, and extension.

*E-mail address*

*Lead owner*—Name of rep who is directly responsible for

calling on this person. Typically, this is the name of the telemarketer until the lead has been contacted and qualified. When it is transitioned to the outside rep, that person becomes the lead owner.

*Do not call*—Indicates that person does not want to be called.

*Account history*—Reflects the date, nature, and results of previous contacts. For example: "5/18/06; talked with Mr. Smith; wants call back in 2 weeks."

*Call-back date*—When you should make your next call.

*Status code*—Current priority within the sales cycle. This is one of the most important bits of data you will need.

For example, let's say that you're selling software directly by phone using an online demonstration as part of your sales process. In this case, you might use the following status codes, enabling you to select those prospects most interested in your product.

1 Customer
2 Agreed to buy; waiting for purchase order
3 Completed demo
4 Wants demo
5 Wants more information/call back soon
6 Wants call back later
7 Trying to reach (less than 3 voice mails)
8 Can't reach (left 3 voice mails or more)
9 No call attempted
10 Not interested
11 Out of business/bad contact information

- *Optional Fields*: You may also want to include other fields in your database such as
- Company descriptors such as industry, annual revenue, number of employees, number of locations

- Interest descriptors specifying the product or feature of particular interest
- Decision maker's assistant and phone number
- Cell phone and fax number
- Marketing campaign in which this lead is included
- Lead source such as web, e-mail, or referral

## FUNCTIONALITY

### Do what you want to do.

At the minimum, you need the ability to search and organize your data. For example, if you have call-back dates for each lead, you will want to sort that data by date or search on today's date in order to determine who you should call immediately. Likewise, you may want to identify all the leads with a particular status code or those located in a particular area code.

Coupled with search capability, reporting capability is also essential. From time to time, you may want to print out a call list or generate a paper report for your co-workers.

Two other functionalities are optional but recommended:

1. *Call-back scheduling*—Scheduling follow-up calls in Outlook or through a CRM program can be very helpful. In a typically busy work day, it's easy to forget who to call. If you electronically add the calls to your calendar, the computer will automatically notify you.
2. *Mail merge*—I strongly believe in sending e-mails to prospects after I call them. Those I reach who express interest receive one standard e-mail. Those I can't reach receive another. Both e-mails include attached product information. The simplest way to manage this process is to use the mail merge capacity built into most CRM

applications. While Excel can merge with Word documents, the process is more arduous.

# PART 7

# KNOW YOUR STUFF

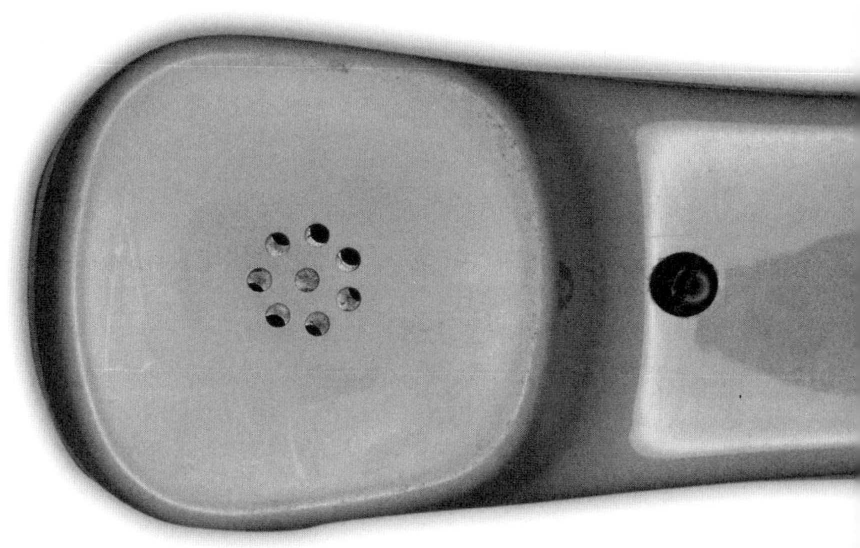

# CHAPTER TWENTY-ONE

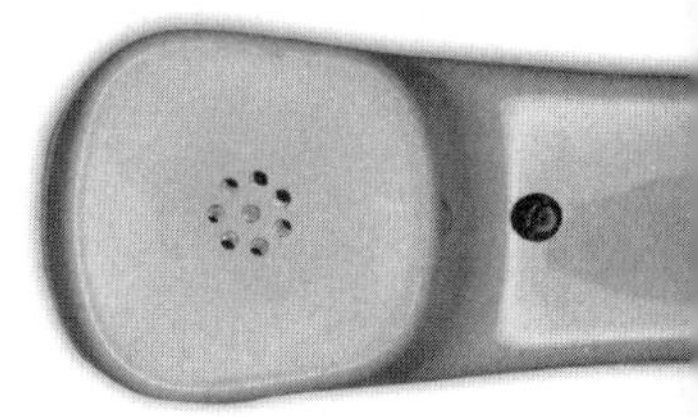

# The semi-expert

EVERY TIME I TALK WITH a client about hiring me for telemarketing, the same question arises, "What do you know about the product (or service) we're selling?" My answer is always the same: "Not much, but I'm a fast learner!"

I explain the obvious: "If you know a product expert who is also a telemarketing expert, you need to hire that person." (Of course, I know they wouldn't be interviewing me if they had already found Mr. Wonderful.)

"If not, you have two choices," I continue matter-of-factly. "You can hire a product expert and teach him to be a telemarketing expert. Or you can hire a telemarketing expert and teach him the product information."

After a sufficient pause, I close by adding, "I think you'll find that it will be much easier to teach me about your product than to teach a product expert what I know about telemarketing!"

Inevitably, they agree.

And so, I start every assignment knowing little or nothing about the product/service I'm selling. In some ways, this is an advantage. I can see the merchandise with a clear, fresh perspective. I can more easily discern the most important features and benefits without being inundated with peripheral details. I can see the product as potential buyers see it, stripped of its glitter, standing alone without position papers and technical manuals, simple and new, ready to serve.

While my product ignorance is often ignored during the interview, it's no excuse after I start making calls. Those I call may be impressed with my style, but they also want substance. Selling the sizzle without the steak can only take you so far. And so, my first task on a new job is to cram myself full of facts and figures about the product's features, benefits, competitive advantage, and all the other important details.

Even so, I remember that I'm never going to know as much about the product I'm selling as the people who designed it or who service it. (And they're never going to know as much about selling it over the phone as I do.) What's important is that I know the most important facts, the information that will satisfy 95 percent of the people I call.

If you classify all product information on a 1–10 scale with 10 being every fact known, 75 percent of all telemarketing calls require product knowledge on a level 3, which is basically what the item does and how it will help, summarized in a few sentences. Another 20 percent, involving questions and objections, require level 6–7 knowledge. The remaining 5 percent require expertise beyond my capacity and necessitate help from more knowledgeable members of my team.

Therefore, before you can represent your product adequately, you need to separate the information needed in 95 percent of your calls from the other 5 percent. The more experience you have in telemarketing, the easier this task will be. Unfortunately, you can't rely on other staff members to help you in this quest. Technical experts are so flooded with facts that they can rarely separate which are more important. Fellow sellers who use the dump-every-fact-you-know-on-the-poor-unsuspecting-customer strategy won't be of any help either.

Rely on your own best judgment to determine information priorities. Then test your theory in the marketplace. If multiple prospects ask for facts that aren't part of your regular repertoire, add what you're missing. If some of your information gains no traction with most callers, drop it. Gradually, you'll determine what potential buyers want to hear. And when you do, repeat what you've learned again and again.

In the end, you'll sound like an expert without being too bogged down in obscure facts and figures.

## FEATURES

### Know what it does and how it does it.

Start by looking at the product's features. What does it do? How does it do it? Is it a product, a service, or both? How would you describe it in simple, 1-2-3 terms?

I worked briefly for a local software company selling a product that I could never really comprehend. The company describes its product as

" . . . a business process management solution to a company's business needs beginning with business goals alignment with an eye toward creating business value through process change."

Do you want that with fries? I'm sure some people understand what they're selling. I'm just not one of them. Needless to say, I got fired when they learned that I didn't understand—and frankly, didn't want to understand—what they were talking about.

Fuzzy-sounding products have their place in the big world, but they don't lend themselves well to telemarketing. As discussed earlier, the telemarketer only has a few seconds to convey the most important information. It would take me an hour to explain all that mumbo jumbo. Long before then, I'd be listening to the phone click off on the other end.

Identify the three most important features of your product. Then describe each in straightforward, commonsense terms using active verbs and short sentences.

> "No one can remember more than three points."
>
> —Philip Crosby

## BENEFITS

### Explain why it's important.

As discussed earlier, a dancing refrigerator may be a marvelous invention, but why would anyone buy one?

Knowing the features of your product is important. Understanding its benefits is essential. What needs does this product fulfill? What problems does it solve? Will the buyer be richer, safer, or happier as a result of having this invention?

Many people confuse features and benefits. Perhaps they assume that because a product does XYZ a buyer will immediately recognize the value of having it. For example, I'm always skeptical of "bells and whistles" added to new software versions, particularly when I'm perfectly happy with the old model. Things that are working perfectly well become so "new and improved" that I can't use them any more. Look on the "Help" index of most software programs, and you see a myriad of special features that you'll never use. Unfortunately, some product developers believe in the "build it and they will come" theory, assuming that new things are inherently beneficial. The dot-com bust illustrated how expensive this kind of thinking can be.

A complex product or service may offer a variety of benefits. Identify the most important one(s). For example, if you're selling a pill that cures cancer, the product has two benefits: (1) it saves your life, and (2) it's convenient to take. Obviously, one benefit is a great deal more important than the other. The other consideration in prioritizing benefits is the opinion of the decision maker. What is important to the receptionist may not be important to the CEO.

Once you've identified the primary benefit(s), formulate a sentence that will describe it clearly. Use simple and direct words that the listener will immediately understand. Forget the jargon and business-speak. If your product will increase company revenue, say so, in just those words. Explaining benefits is like explaining jokes. If the listener doesn't get it immediately, explaining the punch line won't help.

## OBJECTIONS

### Prepare to respond.

As discussed later, objections typically fall into one of these categories:

1. No need
2. No money
3. No time
4. No trust
5. No authority

To respond to objections, you need two tools: (1) a probing question designed to expose the exact nature of the problem/concern, and (2) a standard compelling response that addresses the problem/concern. Draft and practice these scripted responses before you begin calling.

> "When I prepare for a sales presentation, I try to think like my client and like my competitor. I try to pinpoint every objection that either of them could make to my presentation. I write these objections down, and then I figure out a way to respond to each one in three lines or less."
>
> —Mark Jarvis

## CUSTOMER SERVICE

### Outline what happens next.

What can customers expect after the sale? Who will help with the product's installation and start-up? How long will it take? What internal resources must be provided by the customer? Who, when, and how will product training be conducted? Look beyond the sale. Walk the buyer through each step following his signature on the dotted line. If your company's customer service is responsive, knowledgeable, and caring, emphasize that advantage. If it's not, sell for somebody else.

## LEGAL AND SAFETY

### Warn responsibly.

Critical legal and safety issues should be discussed at the outset to ensure that the buyer has all the necessary facts in order to make an informed decision. Explain possible safety hazards and liability issues.

## PRICE

### Tell them how much.

If you're selling a product directly, talking about price is a necessary part of the sales process. But if you're generating leads for an outside salesperson, money discussions are best left to the rep. The more expensive the product, the more wiggle room is built into pricing—room that the rep will use to close the deal.

Even so, have a ball park idea of price when you make calls. Having no idea of pricing, or at least pretending that you don't, makes you look stupid and powerless, like the hapless car salesman who has to keep checking with the hidden sales manager for the "best offer." To be safe, offer a wide but reasonable price range; and specify the details that determine the final number.

I've heard the expression that if you have to ask the price, you can't afford it. For the most part, I've found this to be true in selling more expensive products and services. Decision makers with small budgets are likely to ask about price in an initial telemarketing call. Those with money are looking for the best value (not necessarily the lowest price) and are unlikely to ask "How much?" until later. When asked, offer a price range, not only to establish your credibility, but also to scare away the tire kickers.

## TECHNICAL TERMS

### Speak the language.

Every industry has its technical terms. The successful telemarketer determines which technical terms are essential and which are best left to product experts behind the scenes. For example, when I sold hospital software, I talked about the security of patient data. As anyone knows who has visited a medical professional lately, certain federal regulations called HIPPA (Health Information Portability Protection Act) require caregivers to protect your medical information. Therefore, when asked about this issue, I told decision makers that our software exceeded HIPPA requirements and gave a few technical specifications illustrating that compliance. Occasionally, a security nut would want to know more, like encryption protocols, and so forth. At that point, I got our product security guru to answer his questions.

## COMPETITIVE ADVANTAGE

### Explain why you're better.

Virtually every company has at least one competitor, and if it doesn't today, it will tomorrow. That's the nature of free enterprise. To succeed, you need a "competitive advantage," one or more reasons why the customer would prefer to buy your product from your company than buy from someone else. Maybe it's location, price, service, or reputation. Maybe your product has more features or generates fewer long-term problems than another. Whatever your advantage might be, it's critical that you communicate it to the buyer.

Many businesses seem to overlook this essential step. Maybe they're remembering their childhood lessons about not being too proud or too critical of others. Maybe they believe that their advantages are so obvious that they don't need to be spoken. Maybe they don't have a competitive advantage and hope no one will notice.

You're always selling against the competition, whether you realize it or not. If you're lucky, the prospective client will tell you that he is considering a competitive product and invite you to compare the two. In most cases, the competition is unspoken. The buyer may actually be considering a specific alternative to your offering or may just plan to look into competitive products before he makes a final decision.

If you have a high-quality product, be proactive about discussing its advantages. Give the buyer a set of criteria that he should consider in making a buying decision. Then explain why your specific product is superior based on these factors. By framing the comparison for the buyer, he's more likely to see things from your perspective.

"I am easily satisfied with the very best."

—Winston Churchill

# CHAPTER TWENTY-TWO

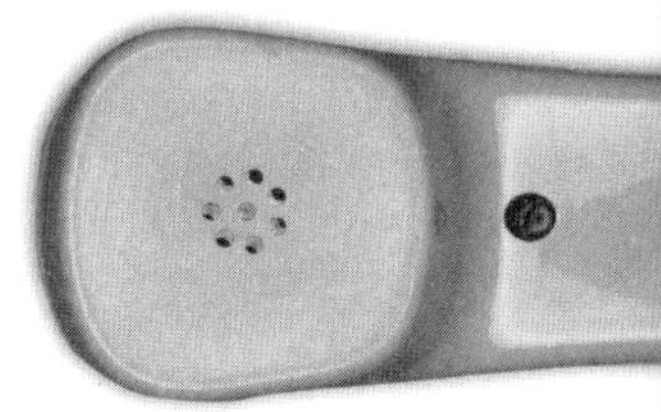

# Back-up

THEORETICALLY, YOU SHOULD BE PREPARED for any contingency before you make the first call. In reality, there's also some weirdo or unexpected questions. Even so, arm yourself with cheat sheets, back-up experts, and collateral material.

## CHEAT SHEETS

### Don't get caught.

In school, teachers tend to frown on writing answers on your wrist or glancing at cheat sheets hidden strategically in your underwear. In telemarketing, you can peek at the answers any time you want. Nobody can see you. Nobody cares!

Print an 8½ x 11" sheet listing the primary features of your product, using a large bold typeface with multiple spaces between the items. Then print a sheet for benefits, another for competitive advantages, and so on, until you have all the most important points condensed in black and white. Then post them at eye level somewhere nearby.

Even if you think you know everything about a product, cheat sheets are still essential. The problem is that you get so involved in a conversation—asking good questions, offering brilliant answers, anticipating objections, and trying to close—that you forget the details of what you're selling. You may remember two benefits, but forget the one that means most to a particular caller. You may be asked why your product is better than the next guy's and draw a complete blank.

Without cheat sheets, you can become a drowning man, frantically grabbing for the few facts you need to keep afloat. I even tape my business card on the computer monitor in case I forget the company name or phone number. Nothing says "Stupid!" like forgetting who you are.

## EXPERTS

### Know who knows what.

When you hear a question you can't answer, don't panic and don't lie. Simply say, "I don't know the answer to that question, but I know someone who does. Let me check with our technical people, and I'll be back to you within twenty-four hours."

I've never known a buyer to protest this approach. If the person does criticize you for being product-stupid, look at the situation objectively. Is this unknown fact something I should have known? If so, learn it, and sin no more. But if, after honest self-examination, you decide that the fact does not need to be cluttering your feeble brain, forget the complainer. You don't need his money that bad.

Assemble a team of experts who can answer those questions that you cannot. This would include a technician who knows every detail about the inner-workings of your gizmo or service, someone who can so overwhelm the questioner with technical tidbits that the person will never question your company's credibility in the future. You also need a marketing expert who can answer detailed questions about competitive products and a customer service expert who can detail the intricacies of the implementation and follow-up process.

Depending on the need, you may want your expert to call or e-mail the buyer directly, or simply to coach you on the details. Regardless, always get back to the questioning person within twenty-four hours after the question was posed. Either answer the question or offer a date when you will answer it.

## COLLATERAL MATERIAL

### Send something impressive after the call.

You need something to send to prospects after you speak with them. In some cases, this may simply be an e-mail with a link to your website. But in other cases, where you may be targeting a particular vertical market or promoting a particular new feature, you may want to attach a PDF file to a follow-up e-mail or mail a copy via USPS.

Remember that the collateral item represents you. If it looks unprofessional, you, your product, and your company will be perceived as unprofessional. If the piece is printed in black & white instead of color, you'll be seen as low-end and old-school. If the material is boring and unattractive to the eye, potential buyers will see you—and your product—in the same way.

Remember that impressions are often more powerful than facts. Like the expression about a picture speaking a thousand words, the buyer's impression of your collateral may last long after he/she has forgotten what you say.

Regarding text, keep it simple. Don't try to explain every feature or benefit. Don't try to anticipate every objection.

Convey a simple memorable message.

In designing sales literature, remember that most people read in newspaper style, starting with the main headline, moving to smaller headlines, moving to the first paragraph of an interesting story, moving to the rest of the text in that article. It's progressive, moving from large to small, simple to more complex. If the headline doesn't grab you, you won't get to the details. If the pictures don't grab you, you won't read the words.

In addition to PDF files, I've also found interactive CDs to be particularly valuable. For example, when selling medical software, I found it nearly impossible to reach physicians directly by phone. So I sent a personalized cover letter, a multi-color PDF, and a CD in a thin blue cover via 2nd day UPS. On the third day, I called each physician's gatekeeper to follow-up. The technique generated a series of return calls.

# PART 8

## SOUND POWER

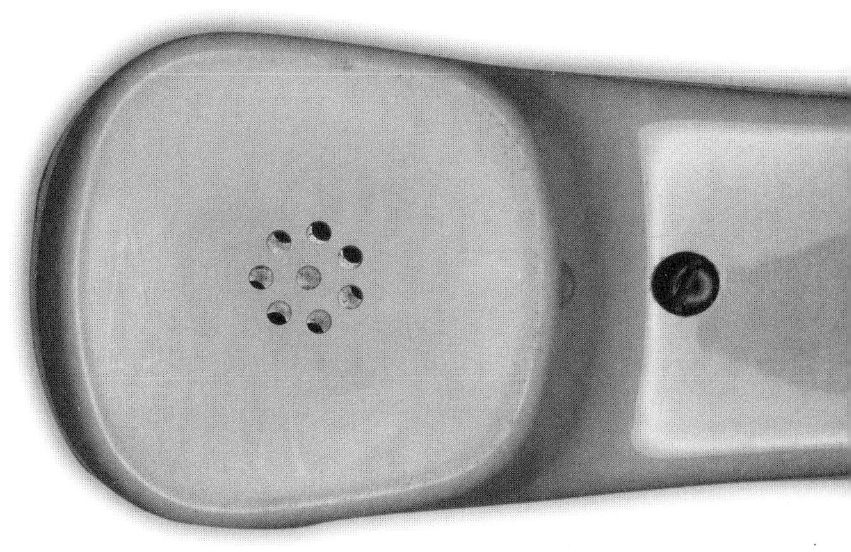

# CHAPTER TWENTY-THREE

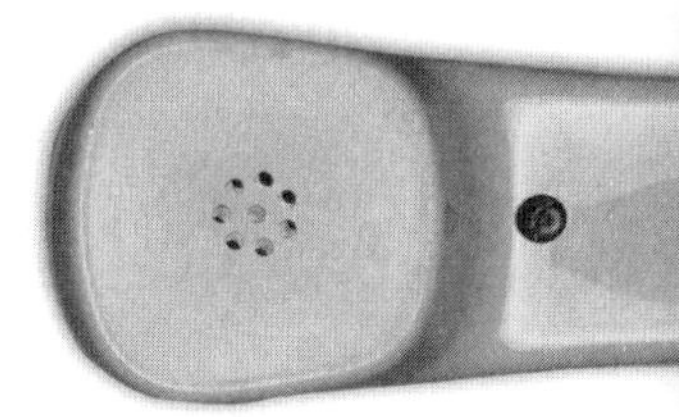

# Use the Force, Luke

I REMEMBER WALKING OUT OF the first Star Wars movie in awe. Incredible space ships, Darth Vader, lightsabers, wow! It was seriously cool! But it was more than an adventure story. It was a spiritual story too, about something called "The Force."

As Obi-Wan explains, "The Force is an energy field created by all living things that surrounds us, and penetrates us, and binds the galaxy together."

Those who are "strong with the Force" can move heavy objects, fight with superhuman strength, and manipulate the minds of the weak. Do you remember that scene where Luke, Obi-Wan, and the droids were stopped by stormtroopers in the Tatooine spaceport?

Stormtrooper: *Let me see your identification.*

Obi-Wan: [*with a small wave of his hand*] *You don't need to see his identification.*

Stormtrooper: *We don't need to see his identification.*

Obi-Wan: *These aren't the droids you're looking for.*

Stormtrooper: *These aren't the droids we're looking for.*

Obi-Wan: *He can go about his business.*

Stormtrooper: *You can go about your business.*
Obi-Wan: *Move along.*
Stormtrooper: *Move along . . . move along.*

In the telemarketing world, tone of voice is "The Force." It may not enable you to lift heavy objects or be a super-strong warrior, but it will allow you to influence the minds of others, weak and otherwise.

## IN THE BEGINNING

### Commune with the divine.

Starting with the grunts and growls of prehistoric beings, sound has always had a powerful effect on human beings. Throughout the centuries, major religions and native cultures have included songs and chants in their ceremonies as a way to "enter into a dialogue with the divine."

In yoga, repeating mantras (simple phrases derived from the Sanskrit alphabet) is thought to concentrate and intensify consciousness. Likewise, toning (the continuous sounding of a syllable like "OH") is said to synchronize brainwaves, relieve tension, and restore harmony to mind and body. The ability of music around the world to evoke a full range of human emotions testifies to the universal power of sound.

One yoga master describes the power of chanting this way:

"Chanting is a natural way to tune in to the frequency of love. Chanting combines singing and music with mantras—words and sounds that vibrate at the highest level of awareness. The vibrations emanating from repeating the names of God or chanting sacred Sanskrit texts have a tangible effect on our own inner being. The sweetness of chanting stills the mind, dissolves worries, and opens the heart. The saints describe chanting as a way of becoming saturated with God's love."

Some believe that sound has unique healing properties. According to Simon Healther (*The Healing Power of Sound*):

"Sound has been used as a healing force for thousands of years. All ancient civilizations used sound for healing. Traditional cultures still surviving today understand the remarkable healing power that lies in sound.

"In the Bible we are told that David played his harp to lift King Saul's depression. Egyptian papyri over 2,600 years old refer to incantations as cures for infertility and rheumatic pain.

"The ancient Greeks believed music had the power to heal body and soul. They used the flute and the lyre for treating illnesses such as gout and sciatica. It is reported that Alexander the Great's sanity was restored by music played on the lyre.

"When an opera singer vibrates a glass with their voice, they have matched the resonant frequency of the glass. As the singer increases the volume of their sound, the resonance becomes too great for the forces that hold the glass together and it shatters. Modern medicine now uses sound waves to break up kidney stones and gallstones.

"Every organ, every bone, every cell in the body has its own resonant frequency. Together they make up a composite frequency like the instruments of an orchestra. When one organ in the body is out of tune it will affect the whole body. Through sound healing it may be possible to bring the diseased organ into harmony with the rest of the body, hence avoiding the need for drugs or surgery.

"Don Campbell, in his book *The Mozart Effect*, shows

how music, particularly Mozart's, has all kinds of beneficial effects for human health. Scientists suggest that listening to Mozart helps us to improve our powers of concentration and enhances our ability to make intuitive leaps, by organizing the firing pattern of neurons in the cerebral cortex."

## TONES

### Remember: They're more powerful than words.

At one time or another, every child has heard a parent say, "Don't take that tone of voice with me!" No matter how innocent we were trying to be, our tone always gave us away.

Professor Albert Mehrabian, who pioneered the study of nonverbal communication, determined that in typical face-to-face communication, only 7 percent of the meaning is conveyed by the spoken word, with 55 percent coming from body language (facial expression, posture, etc.), and the remaining 38 percent coming from how the words are spoken. In telephone communications, he theorized that only 16 percent of the messaging is verbal (words).

Several studies illustrate the significance of nonverbal messages in personal and professional settings:

- Researchers at the University of Toronto found that the lullabies sung by parents with their babies in the same room sound significantly different than the same lullabies sung by the same people in an empty room. There seems to be a special voice, usually higher in pitch and slower in pace, reflecting the emotions that parents feel when they are physically close to their children.
- Studies have found that when poor medical outcomes occur, surgeons who sounded more dominant and indifferent were more likely to be sued than those who

sounded more concerned and less dominant.

- When judges know that a defendant has a past criminal record, they are more likely to sound cold and impatient toward the individual, increasing the likelihood of conviction, even when the actual prior offenses were never mentioned in court.

"You can say the right thing about a product and nobody will listen. You've got to say it in a way that people will feel it in their gut."

—William Bernbach

# CHAPTER TWENTY-FOUR

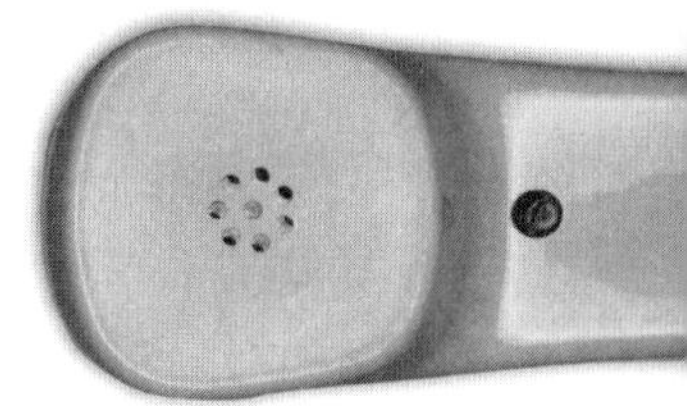

# Harmonic Conversion

THE KEY TO A POWERFUL tone of voice is harmony, the blending of musical notes into a pleasing, relaxing river of sound. While researchers have learned that individuals may differ in defining which specific sounds are harmonious, each of us senses harmony and responds to it in a positive way. When we hear harmonious voices or participate in harmonious relationships, we feel safer, more relaxed, more peaceful, and more open to others.

Think of voices that have calmed you in the past. Remember a parent who comforted you after a bad dream, or a kind teacher who helped you understand a confusing subject. Their voices were low and soft in tone—not whispers or dramatic bass notes—but strong, steady, harmonious beacons of sound.

To find your harmonious voice, hum at a pitch that seems most comfortable. Hum with your mouth closed and listen to the vibrations inside your head. Over time you'll sense the harmonic "Force" of your own voice that can travel undetected into the receptive mind of the customer.

## LOUDNESS

### Control the volume.

Measured in decibels, loudness is technically a measure of the intensity or power with which the sound is emitted. However, loudness is also a function of human perception, related to the physical characteristics of a person's ears and the processing of his brain. What's too loud to one listener may be just right for another.

The chart below illustrates the decibels of common sounds. At 130 Hz, for example, the human ear begins to experience pain.

Table 5

| Sound | Loudness (dB) | Sound | Loudness (dB) |
|---|---|---|---|
| Rustle of leaves | 10 | Motorcycle | 90 |
| Whispering | 20 | Tube train | 100 |
| Ticking watch at 1m | 30 | Pneumatic drill | 110 |
| Quiet street | 40 | Thunder | 120 |
| Quiet conversation | 50 | Building site | 120 |
| Busy office | 60 | Jet takeoff | 140 |
| Loud conversation | 70 | Rifle | 160 |
| Slamming door | 80 | Rocket | 200 |

The loudness or volume of your voice affects customers in both a physical and emotional manner. For example, when a telemarketer speaks too loudly, the sound physically irritates the eardrums so much that the listener pulls the telephone receiver away and subconsciously decides that the caller is obnoxious and untrustworthy. Likewise, in the case of someone who speaks too softly, the listener strains to understand the message and quickly comes to believe that the caller must be hiding something. Either way, the sound of the message becomes more important than its content.

Remember that the listener's—not your—perception of volume is what counts. The best way to learn the appropriate volume on the phone is to call a colleague or family member who can offer immediate, honest feedback. Also, remember that the volume of your voice in a face-to-face situation may not be appropriate for the telephone. The loudness perceived by the listener is affected by how close your mouth is to the receiver, the background noise in or around your office, and the telephone equipment you're using.

Finally, listen to any changes in your loudness during the call. One of my bad habits is to talk louder and louder when a prospect expresses interest in what I'm selling. I'm so excited to reach a "live one" (after a day of leaving voice mails and hearing rejections) that my enthusiasm gushes out. I want to shout "Hurrah!" and dance in the streets. I want the prospect to know how happy I am that he likes what I'm selling and that he likes me!

Unfortunately, too much enthusiasm—like too much sugar in your coffee—can turn the delicious into the undrinkable. Buyers expect and appreciate a certain amount of enthusiasm from the seller when a buying decision is made. But when the seller seems too happy, the buyer begins to wonder why. Does the sales rep sell so few products that this particular transaction is extraordinary? And if his sales are so limited, why doesn't he sell more? Is there something wrong with the product? Is there something wrong with him?

The other problem with talking louder as interest increases is that prospects may mistake enthusiasm for an attempt at dominance. At one time or another, we've all experienced having someone in authority "raise their voice" in order to control our behavior. Maybe it was a parent, a teacher, a boss, or a significant other. Regardless of the source, we didn't like it.

## RATE

### Adjust the speed.

English speakers in America speak at an average speed of 150 words per minute. Some studies have found that "superior" speakers have a slower rate of speech, while others indicate that faster speakers are considered more persuasive. The contradictions are apparent when one considers that FDR spoke at an average rate of 100 words/minute, while JFK zoomed along at 180 words/minute.

Optimal speaking rates also vary by geographic area. As a North Carolina boy calling prospects in big cities up North, I've learned that some folks just naturally talk faster than I do ... and sometimes seem a bit irritated that I won't just "get on with it!" Generally, I try to match my rate of speech to the person with whom I'm speaking. If he or she is moving fast, I get on the bus. If the person is plodding along, I plod too. The object is to blend seamlessly into the buyer's world, with as little static and interference as possible.

Scientists estimate that we think three times faster than we speak. This dichotomy has several ramifications. First, your mind is typically racing as you speak, not only examining the words you're saying at that instant, but also thinking about what to say next, whether the listener is actually listening, and personal matters that just pop into your brain. You're trying to stay calm, but you're worried about closing the sale. Considering the mental jumble swirling through your head, you must know your basic script so completely that it can be delivered without thinking. You're like the juggler who can recite the Gettysburg Address, while keeping three balls in the air.

Secondly, it's important to remember that the listener's thoughts are moving faster than your speech. By the time you've explained Point #1, the buyer may be thinking ahead to Point #3. Your words must be so well crafted and your speed so well regulated that the listener is connected to everything you say, neither skipping ahead to what's coming next, or thinking back on what you just said.

Salespeople have a general reputation for being fast talkers, filling empty minds with so many words in such a short time that the customer finds the sales pitch irresistible. This may work for snake oil salesmen, but not for ethical telemarketers interested in long-term business relationships based on trust. The object is not to drown the prospect in verbiage, but to make every word count. The goal is to get the listener to understand and accept a few key concepts, upon which more product detail can be added.

Vary the speed to gain emphasis. Speak fast enough to project enthusiasm, but slow down regularly to enable the listener to absorb what you've said and experience the emotion that your words have evoked. Say the more complicated and important points at a slower pace; say the simpler, more personalized points at a slighter faster pace.

## PITCH

### Hit the notes.

Pitch is a measure of frequency at which the sound waves vibrate, measured in Hertz (Hz). Like loudness, pitch is in the ear of the listener. Two sounds with the same frequency may not be perceived by two different people as having the same pitch. Loudness affects this perception. The louder the sound, the higher the pitch is thought to be.

The male speaking voice averages 125 Hz, ranging from

100 to 150 Hz. For females, the average is 200 Hz, ranging from 175 to 256 Hz. Men's voices are lower in pitch than women's, even when allowing for body size. Middle C on a piano is calculated at 261.6 Hz. and called "C4" (the first note in the fourth octave on the piano).

Cross-culturally, several conclusions can be drawn about tone in human speech:

1. For both men and women, persons with lower pitched voices are perceived as having more authority and strength.
2. Adults use a higher pitch to talk with infants and young children.
3. Men and women use higher tones in greeting each other and in courtship.
4. Speakers use a rising pitch when asking questions.

The Center for Voice Disorders at Wake Forest University conducted a survey of celebrity voices. James Earl Jones and Julia Roberts were judged as having the best overall voices, Fran Drescher as having the worst. Generally, the survey results showed that Americans prefer melodious, relatively low-pitched voices.

In telemarketing, you'll sound irritating and immature if the pitch of your voice is too high. If your pitch is too low, you'll seem slow and unimaginative.

## INTONATION

### Get a rhythm.

Called intonation, variation in pitch affects perception. For example, a study of nonverbal communication at Boise State University found that attorneys with greater pitch and tempo variety were perceived as more friendly. Another study concluded that ascending musical scales are rated as happier and brighter than descending ones.

If your pitch is unchanging in the course of conversation, you'll sound like you're reading a script, or are bored with the whole thing. If your pitch varies too often and too erratically, you'll sound like a psycho.

Unfortunately, many telemarketers speak in lower and lower pitches as they conclude their comments. The effect is to make them seem less and less excited about the product, and more and more apologetic for making the call in the first place. Needless to say, this problem drains whatever excitement the listener might have acquired during the call. Conclude a call with the same energetic, ascending pitch you used when you began it.

To find the right level and variation in pitch, practice in private. Record your voice and listen objectively. Then ask others to listen and offer feedback. Experiment until you find a consistent range that seems comfortable to say and pleasing to the listener.

Knowing when to pause is just as important as knowing what to say. Without pauses, everything we say is one long sentence, merely a bucket of words without meaning and without influence. Without pauses, the listener has no opportunity to swallow your message and open his mouth for another bite.

Punctuation is the most common indicator that a pause is due. The period at the end of a sentence signals a slight hesitation before the next sentence begins. Commas play the same role within sentences, signaling the need to pause between phrases.

A pause is also valuable after delivering a major section of a script. For example, after you explain who you are and what company you represent, pause before explaining what you sell. If you're listing the major benefits of your product, pause after each. The goal is to provide dramatic emphasis to your message and allow the buyer to absorb that message before hearing the next one.

Waiting too long between sentences, phrases, or script sections will make you sound stilted and unsure. Pauses that are too brief are, in some ways, worse than no pauses at all. They tease and ultimately aggravate the listener who cannot seem to catch his breath as you sprint down the field.

During conversations, pauses serve additional purposes. Remember when your father was reminding you to do something you already knew you should do but didn't want to do? He'd just say your name, followed by a long pause: "Stewart! . . ." There was no mistaking what that silence meant.

Another example of a conversational pause is the non-answer to a question. You ask: "Do you understand what I'm trying to say?" The other person says nothing, which could mean that he or she (1) doesn't understand, (2) is too irritated with you to answer, or (3) is too intimidated to say anything. Regardless, those few seconds of silence speak volumes.

Generally, when a prospect says nothing after your presentation, it is an indication that the person is considering your words and wants to know more. This is the perfect time to ask a question, because the listener is already asking some type of question in his own mind, like: "Will this work with our existing system?" "Can this company really be trusted?" "Can I afford it?" and so on.

Ask an open-ended question such as, "What do you think?" or "Do you think this might of some help to you?" The first words out of the buyer's mouth will probably indicate that person's primary concern.

## FLUENCY

### Speak smoothly.

Researchers define fluency as "speech that is free of long pauses, hesitations, repetitions, and extraneous vocal sounds such as 'um' or 'hmmm.'" In a study of attorneys' opening statements, J. K. Barge and Associates found that lawyers with a fluent style were considered more competent and dynamic than those without.

The key to selling on the telephone is developing trust with the listener, and the key to developing trust is to approach the buyer naturally and without pretense, like a friendly new neighbor. Even though you are delivering the same script over and over again, the words don't sound scripted. They sound natural and friendly, effortless and smooth. You're not stumbling and bumbling over awkward phrases or high tech terminology. You're not thinking about what to say; because the words, the phrasing, the pauses, the emphasis . . . everything you say and the way you say it have been so fine-tuned and so thoroughly rehearsed that they flow like water into the ears of the buyer.

## ENUNCIATION

### Say it distinctly.

Say each word distinctly, without sounding formal. Devote particular attention to the beginning and ending sounds. Finish saying word one before starting to say word two. Insert a minisecond pause between each word as needed, but don't extend the pauses too long. Speak so clearly that the listener understands every word. The trick is to sound intelligent, without sounding snobby.

The words you emphasize within a given sentence can vastly change how the buyer perceives your meaning. A company called *American Accent Training* uses the following examples in training outsourced telemarketers how to speak standard American English:

Consider how a sentence's meaning changes as different words are emphasized:

- *I* didn't say he stole the money, someone else said it.
- I *didn't* say he stole the money, that's not true at all.
- I didn't *say* he stole the money, I only suggested the possibility.
- I didn't say *he* stole the money, I think someone else took it.
- I didn't say he *stole* the money, maybe he just borrowed it.
- I didn't say he stole *the* money, but rather some other money.
- I didn't say he stole the *money*; he may have taken some jewelry.

> "Speak clearly, if you speak at all; carve every word before you let it fall."
>
> —Oliver Wendell Holmes

## PRONUNCIATION

### Sound it out.

Decision makers are not impressed when you mispronounce their names, company names, technical terms, or any other words that they consider important. To avoid mispronouncing the name of an individual, call the company and ask the receptionist to pronounce it for you. Write it down phonetically as she/he says it. Next, repeat the name over and over to yourself until it falls effortlessly from your lips. Then call back, ask the receptionist for the individual by name (as a dress rehearsal), and then address the person correctly when he or she answers. The decision maker will appreciate it.

## VARIATIONS

### Watch that accent, ya'll.

I'm told that I have a Southern accent. I don't hear it, but I do notice that folks in other parts of the country talk funny. I like my accent. I think it sounds friendly and laid-back, likeable qualities in a salesperson. However, I am careful to avoid sounding like a good-ole-boy or a country hick . . . unless, of course, I'm selling to those folks.

Most businesspeople, both in and out of the South, think that too much of a Southern accent implies that the speaker is stupid. I prefer to avoid that moniker. Accents have limitations. Too much Yankee-ese sounds harsh and unfriendly. Too much Texas cowboy sounds unprofessional. Customer service operators in India speak English, but many have such a strong Indian accent that I can't understand them.

Like it or not, "standard English" is the language of business. While decision makers will tolerate a moderate degree of regional or foreign accent by a telemarketer, they will reject a caller who sounds radically different from their perception of proper speech, which is usually defined as the way people sound on television. VIPs are most impressed by callers who have the same accents as they do.

## WARMTH

### Spread the sunshine.

Business can be cold and unforgiving . . . dog-eat-dog, take-no-prisoners, struggle for the almighty dollar. Whether they realize it or not, decision makers need human warmth, a ray of summer sun on an otherwise dreary winter day. Offering that warmth in your phone conversation is both a good deed and an effective selling tool.

Think of the buyer as a friend with a problem. One day you discover that you have the solution to that problem. So you call your friend on the phone, excited and happy that you can ease the burden. You look forward to hearing the person's voice, because you know he will welcome what you have to say. You feel good about yourself because you're helping. Your voice exudes genuine concern. The warmth is obvious in your tone. You make a connection with your friend that brightens his day and yours.

The point about warmth is that you can't fake it. If you don't believe that you're helping the buyer, you won't sound warm. If you don't believe in yourself, you won't sound warm. If you hate your job, your product, or your life in general, you certainly won't sound warm. Only through a positive passion about life and its possibilities can you bring a ray of sunshine into the buyer's otherwise cold world.

A cheerful, positive tone can melt the ice in telemarketing. Decision makers feel more comfortable with happy people than sad ones. Don't try to be the slap-on-the-back used car salesman gushing with an ear-to-ear grin. That's hokey and irritating. Don't tell a joke unless you're really good at it, and the joke is generic enough and clean enough to be funny to most people. If the contact person asks how you are, don't say something extreme such as, "If I felt any better, I wouldn't know what to do with myself!" One way to express cheerfulness on a subtle level is to raise the pitch of your voice at the end of a sentence while saying a supportive word. For example, if the VIP asks you if you can do XYZ (and you can), answer "Sure!" or "Absolutely!" with a rising pitch. The key is sincerity. If you feel particularly depressed at a given time, make calls another day.

Ironically, making multiple cold calls can be a depressing experience, especially when no one seems interested in what you're selling. The more calls you make (without success), the more angry and desperate you're likely to feel—which is exactly the opposite attitude you need. In order to sell (or fish) successfully, you must believe that the next call (or the next cast) is going to hook the big one. It's like flipping coins. No matter how many tails you get in a row, there's still a 50/50 chance that you'll get heads on the next flip. In fact, if you let your logical mind wander a bit, you can come to believe that after multiple failures the odds are in your favor.

With this kind of harmless delusion, you can convince yourself to be cheerful with every call. After all, you're going to sell something, guaranteed! It's just a matter of time!

## ENERGY

### Turn it on.

Nothing happens without energy. The most wonderful machine is just a hunk of junk until it's plugged in. The most inspirational ideas are just words until someone decides to act on them. Your product is just another distraction until the buyer gets excited about it.

Like moths, human beings are drawn to the flame of inspiration and passion. They are waiting for someone to turn on the light and show them a better, happier, brighter way.

Sound energetic on every call. Focus your passion and exhibit your intensity without overwhelming the customer.

Don't rely on grandiose phrases and a loud voice to convey your energy. Remember, lightning may be electricity, but it's too dangerous to handle. Edison didn't invent electricity. He found a way to make it useful.

The energy in your call reflects more than your enthusiasm for your product or service. It reflects your attitude toward life. Are you excited to be alive? Are you happy about who you are? Are you hopeful about the future? Selling is more than a well rehearsed act. It's a reflection of who you are.

Imagine you're a prophet, filled with spiritual energy. You speak in a calm, yet powerful voice. Your words are simple, yet your intensity is undeniable. Your voice is a vibrant musical instrument profoundly touching each listener. You teach and inspire. You lead. You serve. You sell.

> "For every sale you miss because you're too enthusiastic, you will miss a hundred because you're not enthusiastic enough."
>
> —Zig Ziglar

# CHAPTER TWENTY-FIVE

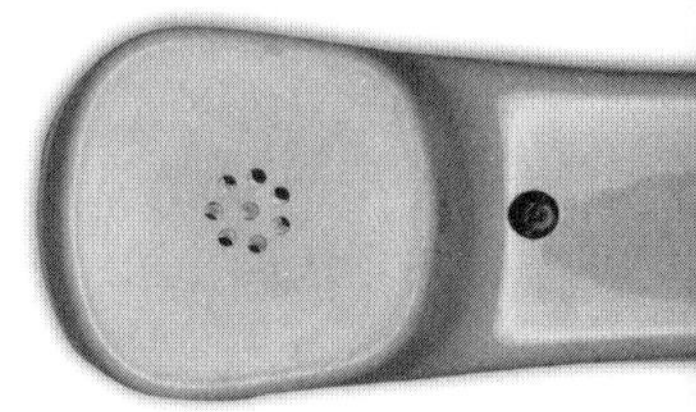

# Interference

YOU'RE AT THE MOVIES WATCHING a great flick. Suddenly, the picture goes out of focus. You try to ignore it, but can't. After a few minutes, all you can think about is the blurry picture and how angry you are that someone hasn't fixed it yet. By that time, the connection you've established with the film is broken. The magic is gone, and you're ready to go home.

A powerful telemarketer and a powerful movie have much in common. Both have the ability to interrupt the viewer or listener's normal routine and transport the person to a new reality, at least for a limited period. But when the image becomes blurred or the sound becomes irritating, that magical connection is broken.

Acoustical situations that can distract the listener can be divided into two groups: connection problems and nonverbal problems.

## CONNECTIONS

### Avoid distractions.

*Background noise*—I've never been hypnotized, but from what I can tell, the process involves entering into a relaxed state of attention and becoming more susceptible to suggestion. The same can be said of telemarketing. You want the person you're calling to relax and focus solely on your voice, an impossibility when there are other voices and extraneous noises in the background.

If you have a private office, close the door before you dial. If you don't, make sure that you are sufficiently insulated from co-workers. Nothing says "boiler room rip-off artist" quite as clearly as the sound of chattering operators in the background.

Ask others in the office to keep their conversations to a dull roar. Recently, I was in the middle of a call when several of the production folks on the other side of the room burst out laughing. They were at least 50 feet away, but the guy I was talking to heard them and immediately said, "Sounds like you're having fun over there!" Even an amateur hypnotist knows that you can't cast a spell when people are hollering from the peanut gallery.

*Cell phones*—Don't use them for cold calling. The technology creates a somewhat muffled, distant sound that is easily recognizable by the person being called. From the listener's perspective, the telemarketer who uses a cell phone doesn't have a real office and, therefore, doesn't represent a real company.

*Echo/static*—Occasionally, your landline connection will sound weird, echoing or buzzing with static. Don't try to continue. Tell the listener that you have a bad connection, then hang-up and call back immediately. In 99.99 percent of the cases, you won't have a problem on the redial.

*Headset*—I'm just not a headset kind of guy . . . too old school, I guess. Practically, I'm concerned about the quality of my voice. Like a singer using a microphone on stage, I know how close to hold the phone to my lips and when to adjust that distance based on what I'm saying. If I'm making a dramatic, emphatic point, I tend to talk louder, so I move the phone away. If I'm trying to sound more personal and intimate, I speak softer and move the phone closer. If you're an inexperienced head-setter, practice a few calls with your friends to make sure the volume is right.

*Speakerphone*—Never use a speakerphone in cold calling. It's rude and a serious turnoff for decision makers who want personal, one-on-one attention. When the listener hears the distinctive echo created by this technology, he or she naturally assumes that a group of other people are listening, or that you're some kind of big-shot wannabe with his feet propped up on his desk, or that you're a professional con artist. None of those images are particularly inviting.

## NONVERBAL

### Manage the unpredictable.

*Clearing your throat*—It happens to all of us. You're in the middle of a sentence when, gag, a blob of yuck gets stuck in your throat. You can't talk. You can barely breathe. On the other end of the line the listener is startled, wondering if you need the Heimlich maneuver over the phone. When it happens, immediately cover the phone mike, clear your throat, and go back to the line. Start with a simple, "Excuse me," before resuming the conversation where you left it. If you're lucky, the broken state of attention will return.

*Coughs/sneezes*—Handle these unexpected distractions in the same way. Do it. Apologize. Return to normal before the mood changes.

*Heavy breathing*—You're a nervous wreck. The boss is on your case, your kids are sick, and you really need the next prospect to say "Yes!" So, when Mr. Big answers his phone you find yourself hyperventilating, gasping for air as your head starts to spin. Your breathing is heavy and labored. When this happens, get off the phone ASAP. Catch your breath. Walk around the building. Go to lunch early. E-mail a friend. Sure, work is important, but it's not worth a coronary. Besides, nobody wants to buy from somebody who's going over the edge. Try again later.

*Hiccups*—I've never gotten the hiccups during a call, but I've called someone who couldn't stop. He was an executive with a professional sounding voice and a moderate interest in my product, but he couldn't stop hiccupping every twenty to thirty seconds. At first I ignored the distraction. After a few times, he apologized and I reassured him that I didn't care. After about two minutes we were both going crazy, and decided that I should call back another day. If this affliction suddenly comes over you, immediately excuse yourself from the phone and stick your head in the nearest paper bag.

*Illness*—Don't call if you're sick, particularly if you have a nasal cold. The person on the other end just wants you to quit sniffling and go home for the day.

*Stuttering*—If you stutter regularly, telemarketing may not be the profession for you. But if repeating sounds involuntarily is a rare malady, you can cure yourself by deliberately allowing an extra pause just before you say a sound that is likely to evoke the problem.

# PART 9

## GETTING IN

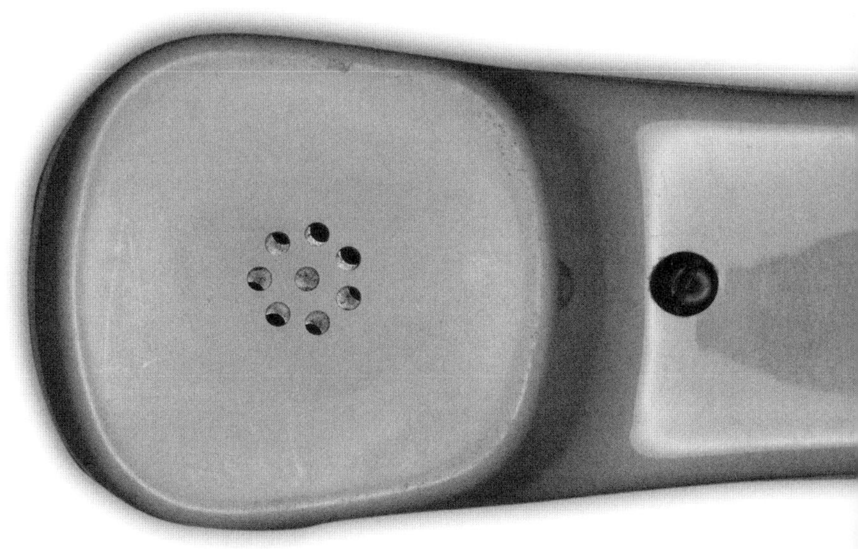

# CHAPTER TWENTY-SIX

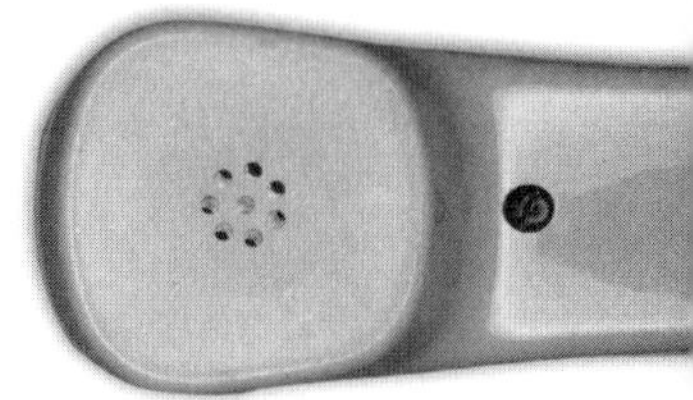

# Direct dial

THE DECISION MAKER LIVES IN a fortified castle, protected by stone walls that seem impenetrable. Guards protect his private chambers and allow no stranger to pass. Even so, a thin wire weaves through the stones, up the tower, past the gatekeepers, and directly to the telephone on his royal desk. All you need is the secret code that will allow your words to travel through the line, undeterred, into the inner sanctum. All you need is the decision maker's direct phone number.

## RESEARCH

### Snoop in public places.

*Company website*—Look at the company's website. Under the section "About Us" or "Management Team," you'll frequently find a listing of the company's senior managers. In some cases a direct phone number will appear beside the leader's name. Get the e-mail address too, if it's available.

If the organization is a public entity like a university or unit of government, you may be able to find a personnel directory on the website. If you don't immediately see the link, type the word "directory" into the "Search" box on the site, typically located in the upper right-hand corner of the home page.

*Google*—Enter the decision maker's name in Google. Often, you'll find the decision maker on a directory of professionals who are part of a group or association. For example, the CIO may be listed with other IT professionals as part of a committee to increase computer access within a given community. Maybe the safety director is listed on a state task force on workplace safety. Look for a phone number.

*Voice mail*—A company's voice-mail system often provides a direct phone number. For example, if you ask the receptionist to connect you to Dan O'Brien, you may hear a recording that says: "The party at extension 1466 is not available at this time," or "This is Dan O'Brien at extension 1466, I'm sorry I'm not here to take your call . . . ."

*Dial by name*—Sometimes the voice-mail system offers a "dial by name directory," in which you enter a few letters of the person's name and press pound. The resulting message says, "You are being connected to Dan O'Brien at extension 1466." If dial by name doesn't include the contact's name, type a common name into the system, like Smith or Jones. Call that person's extension. When he or she answers, apologize for the inconvenience; explain that you're looking for Dan O'Brien; and ask for the correct extension number.

*Sequential dialing*—On a few occasions, I've resorted to sequential dialing in order to get a VIP's direct number. In these cases, I got the direct number for the person's administrative assistant and then dialed the next number in sequence until I reached the right person. For example, if the administrative assistant's extension was 7521, I would try 7522,

7533, and so on—or dial 7520, 7519, and so on—until I succeeded. In the interest of candor, I must admit that this has only worked twice, and in both cases, I sold nothing.

## THE RECEPTIONIST

### When in doubt, ask.

Call the company's main phone number, and ask the receptionist.

You: *Hello! This is Stewart Rogers. How are you?*

Receptionist: *Fine. How can I help you?*

You: *I'm trying to reach Adam Winston. What's his direct number?*

Use a calm, business-like tone, friendly and fearless at the same time. Imagine that it's a beautiful day and you're simply making a happy call to a colleague. To the weary, underpaid, overworked, underappreciated peon who answers the corporate phones, you're a breath of fresh air, a welcome visitor, certainly not a threat. Caught up in your aura and the mood of the moment, the receptionist will, in many cases, give you the extension or direct number.

# CHAPTER TWENTY-SEVEN

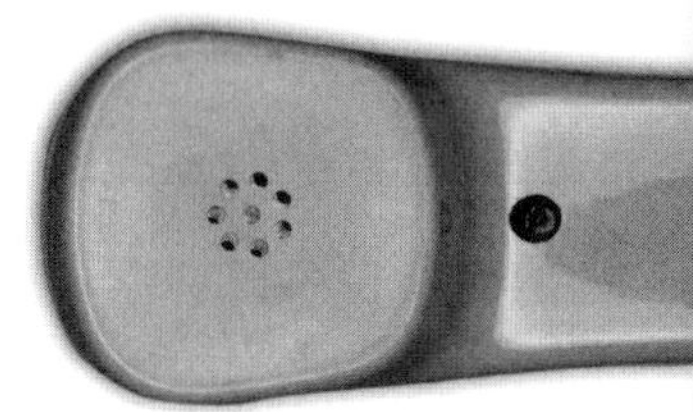

# Gatekeepers

If you can't get the decision maker's direct phone number, you're going to have to deal with a "gatekeeper." Even though these folks are usually mild-mannered, think of them as burly giants standing outside the king's door with the keys in one hand and a club in the other.

## PLAN A
### Fake it.

You may be able to sneak past the gatekeeper by using the "I'm a very important person technique." Start by asking for the decision maker by name, using a pleasant but authoritarian tone-of-voice.

For example, to reach Bill Smith simply say, "Bill Smith, please," using a low, stern, slightly impatient tone—a tone which implies that you are an authority figure of some sort.

To develop this tone, imagine that you are a very important executive. Million dollar deals are everywhere. You're late for a lunch meeting with the CEO of General Motors and don't have time to waste with a mere secretary. You are polite, but cold. Your tone and your words imply that you are giving an order, not asking for permission. You seem nice enough on the surface, but not someone to be messed with.

This voice works best with receptionists and second-tier administrative assistants who are afraid to question you. They would rather transfer your call than embarrass themselves, or incur the wrath of their boss for denying you immediate access.

One of the most common mistakes a telemarketer can make is to ask permission to speak with someone: "May I speak with Mr. Smith?"

While this approach is traditionally polite, it also raises a red flag about the caller's right to speak with Mr. Smith. Remember that you're asking permission from a receptionist or administrative assistant who has little authority except to screen out callers like you. If you have to ask permission, you probably don't deserve access.

In the best case scenario, your call is transferred without questioning or delay. More likely, the gatekeeper may decide to check your passport before waiving you through.

You: *Albert Davis, please.*

Gatekeeper: *Who may I say is calling?*

You: *Janice Williams.*

Sometimes your name is enough information. But usually, the gatekeeper will want to know more, asking for your company name and/or your connection to the decision maker.

Gatekeeper: *And you're with ... ?*

You: *Albertson Electronics.*

Maybe you'll get transferred now. More likely, the gatekeeper will ask a question you don't want to answer:

Gatekeeper: *Is Mr. Davis expecting your call?*

*(or)*

*Will Mr. Davis know what this is about?*

Show no fear. Answer the question briefly and confidently, offering an easily understood benefit that might impress the gatekeeper:

You: *I'm calling about a new product that will lower your company's energy bill by 10 percent. I think it's something that would interest Mr. Davis.*

At this point, the odds of being transferred directly to the decision maker are nil and none. You've identified yourself as a salesperson and implied that you have no previous relationship with the decision maker. Under the circumstances, you'll probably hear:

Gatekeeper: *Mr. Davis doesn't accept sales calls. I can take your name and number, and he'll call you back if he's interested.*

You're caught. There's nowhere to run, nowhere to hide. The only alternative is Plan B.

## PLAN B

### Make a friend.

Plan B involves making the gatekeeper your ally. Lower your expectations and understand that reaching the decision maker will take four steps instead of one.

(1) *Change your demeanor.* Immediately switch from your authoritarian voice to a softer, more conciliatory one. Stop pushing and start charming. Say "Hello" in a happy way, like you were greeting your next door neighbor (whom you like). Sincerely ask: "How are you?" Wait for the answer. Listen for clues to her mood. In my experience, the higher the decision maker is in the organizational structure, the more pleasant his administrative assistant tends to be. Take your time. Relax.

(2) *Explain why you're calling.* Describe what you're selling again in two or three sentences. Be honest and brief. Explain why the boss might be interested, naming high profile references if you have any. Avoid extraordinary claims. If your pitch sounds even a little bit iffy, this sweet lady will cut you off at the knees.

(3) *Ask permission.* Ask the gatekeeper if you can speak briefly with her boss. Emphasize the "briefly" part, saying that you just want to introduce yourself. Make your request sound simple and harmless.

If you've done a superior job of charming the ogre in the door, she will say, "Hold. Let me ask Mr. Davis if he has a minute to talk with you." A very cool offer!

If you're incredibly lucky the gatekeeper will say, "Wow! What a coincidence. Mr. Davis is really interested in this kind of thing. Hold, and I'll transfer you." When that happens, you know the sales gods love you. That's as good as it gets!

(4) *Follow-up.* In 99 percent of the cases the gatekeeper will ask for your name and phone number, and request that you send some information to Mr. Davis for his consideration. If you're moderately lucky, you'll get his personal e-mail address. More likely, you'll get the gatekeeper's e-mail address—or worse still, you'll be asked to send information by mail.

As a general rule, establishing a direct link with the gatekeeper is your best strategy. Ask her if you can send information to her directly. If she agrees, you've at least gotten her working on your side. When you call again, she'll know you personally and may be more inclined to transfer your call into the inner sanctum.

## ACCEPTANCE

### Live with it.

In the end, you must accept what you can't change. If the decision maker wants his assistant to block all calls, she will block all calls, no exceptions. If he prefers that you e-mail, or mail all your information to another person, that's the way it has to be done.

Gatekeepers are incredibly loyal to their bosses, not simply because their jobs depend on it, but because they are honest, trustworthy people who take their responsibilities seriously. They think of themselves as protectors, perhaps in the way a mother might protect a child. In many cases, the decision maker and his assistant have worked together for years, enduring many bumps in the road, fending off hundreds, maybe thousands of pesky salespeople like you. Nothing is going to jeopardize this relationship.

# CHAPTER TWENTY-EIGHT

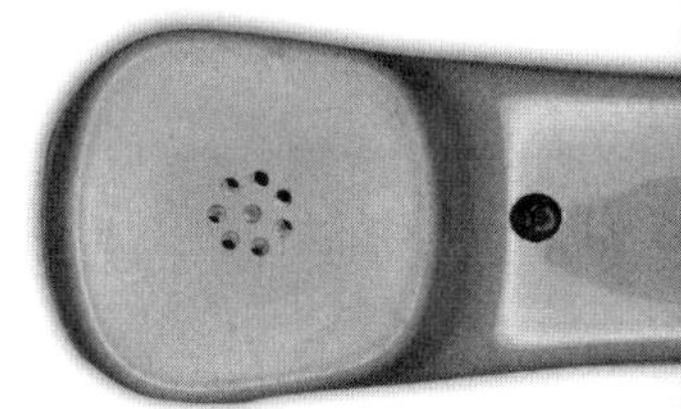

## When to call

THE LIKELIHOOD OF REACHING A decision maker is significantly decreased by calling at the wrong times, including:

- Monday mornings
- The day after a three-day holiday
- The week of Thanksgiving
- The week before and after Christmas
- Between 10:00 a.m. and 11:45 a.m.
- Before 8:00 a.m.

Surprisingly, I've found that Friday afternoons after 3:00 p.m. are often good times to reach VIPs and secure buying decisions. By that time, the week is almost over. Meetings and client calls are typically finished for the day.

The decision maker is looking back over his unfinished business, planning for the next week. He's tired, so he's operating more on gut instinct than clear-headed logic. Buying something would be a fun way to end the day. Solving another problem would be a relief.

You call. You're pleasant and relaxed. You and Mr. Big prop your feet up, so to speak, and connect over a tall one, so to speak. He likes you. He likes what you're selling. He's got no real objections, and the price is OK.

"Why not?" he thinks, and gives you the order.

# PART 10

# WHAT TO SAY

# CHAPTER TWENTY-NINE

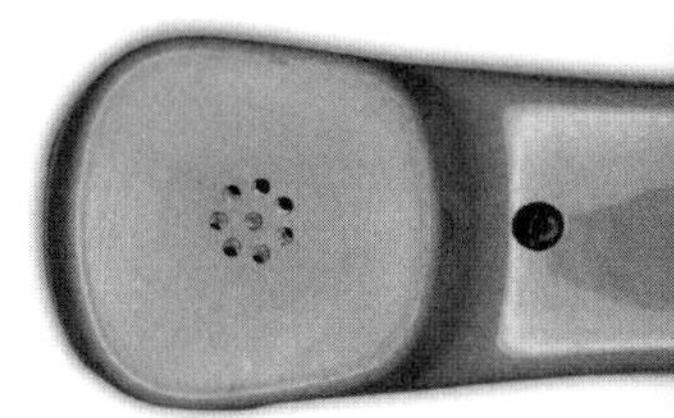

# Winning words

LIKE MOST BOYS, I WAS raised to believe in "pickup lines"—cleverly crafted incantations that would magically compel the fairer sex to make out with you in the back seat of your dad's car. Unfortunately, I never learned what those mystical words actually were. I suppose it's vaguely possible that perfect pickup lines never existed, any more than perfect words exist in telemarketing. But as guys with chicks will tell you, some words work better than others.

This chapter offers words that are more likely to have a favorable effect in the sales process. Toss them around. Put them together. Slip them into the conversation. Find the lines that work best for you.

## THE SWEETEST SOUND

### Name names.

I believe in starting and ending every call by saying the name of the person I'm calling:

*Hello, Bill. How are you?*

*Thanks Bill! I appreciate your time!*

Ninety-five percent of the time I call prospects by their

first names. I try to distinguish between sounding friendly (which I am) and sounding personally close or familiar with the person (which I am not). Operating on a first-name basis from the outset helps me to level the playing field, increasing the tendency of the decision maker to see me more as a partner than a peon, more as a peer than a pest.

I call a physician Dr. (last name), and a chief executive of a particularly large or prestigious enterprise as Mr. or Ms. (last name).

> "Remember that a person's name is to that person the sweetest and most important sound in any language."
>
> —Dale Carnegie

## BEING POLITE

### Remember your manners.

My parents taught me to be polite every time, all the time. But it's more than a habit. It's a way of life that serves as my foundation for selling. I thank people for answering the phone. I thank them for listening. I thank them for asking questions. I thank them for answering my questions. And I thank them—usually several times—for buying.

I try never to forget that, in the beginning, I am a stranger to everyone I call—a homeless, wide-eyed kid standing on the porch, hat in hand, waiting for the front door to open. The person inside is under no obligation to let me in or to hear what I have to say. So, when one of these strangers takes me in and listens to my story, I am sincerely grateful.

The other "magic word," as Mom would say, is "please." Asking someone to do something without first saying "please" is like ordering them to do it. I have no authority to order anybody to do anything. My job is not to force people into buying, but to help them determine whether buying my product is in their best interest.

## SUBLIMINAL "YES"

### Plant a suggestion.

I have developed a habit of saying the word "Yes" before saying anything else. For example:

Dec mkr: *Hello.*

You: *Yes! This is Stewart Rogers. How are you today?*

Starting your spiel by enthusiastically saying the word "Yes," implants a subliminal message into the decision maker's brain, promoting the perception that you are a positive person and that your proposal should be considered favorably.

## TOO MUCH OF A GOOD THING

### Be original.

Factiva, a Dow Jones & Reuters company, analyzed 388,000 news releases from companies in North America and discovered the twenty most commonly used words and phrases, in this order:

Next generation
Flexible
Robust
World class
Scalable
Easy to use
Cutting edge
Well positioned
Mission critical
Market leading
Industry standard
Turnkey

Groundbreaking
Best of breed
Enterprise class
User friendly
Enterprise wide
Interoperable
Extensible
Breakthrough

The question is: If everything is next generation, flexible, and robust, is anything next generation, flexible, and robust? Overworked words are like overworked people: sooner or later, they can't carry the weight.

# CHAPTER THIRTY

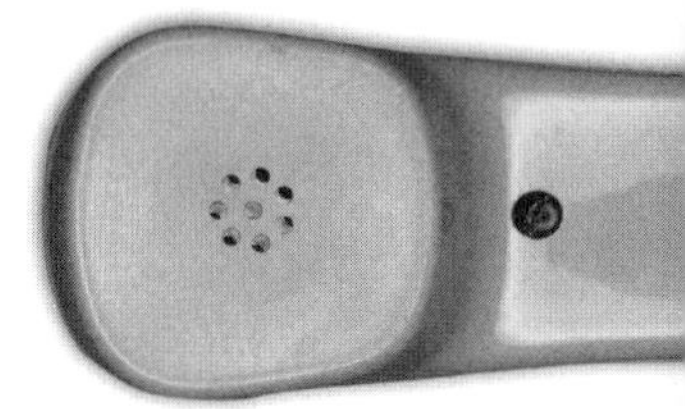

# You had me at hello

DO YOU REMEMBER THE MOVIE *Jerry Maguire?* Tom Cruise is a struggling sports agent who returns to his estranged wife after a long separation. He greets her at the door and begins a long dissertation about his past mistakes. After a prolonged monologue, she interrupts him and says, "You had me at 'hello'!" In sales, a warm, genuine greeting will open a subliminal door into the listener's good graces.

## THE GREETING

### Start on the right foot.

It is the big moment. Your voice is toned. Your goals are set. You understand your product. You know whom to call. And you've dialed the number. And now . . . the phone is ringing.

Suddenly, you're having a panic attack. Your mind is blank. You've forgotten what to say. Maybe you should hang up and try again tomorrow.

Then it happens. The ringing stops. The line clicks. And the decision maker answers the phone. "Hello."

Now what?

Hey . . . be cool! Don't panic. Just say "hello" like the friendly person you are.

*"Hello! This is Stewart Rogers with ABC Computers. How are you today?"*

Some folks want to skip over the greeting and get down to business.

Maybe it's my "suthin' upbringing," but I think it's rude to start selling something before you've even said "Hello." Besides, I've found that starting a conversation in a kind, nonthreatening manner does more to sell my trustworthiness than all the fancy words I can muster.

## THE ANSWER

### Care enough to listen.

When you say, "How are you?" the typical answer is "Fine," or "OK." Listen to the tone in which the answer is given. If it's strong and polite, the listener is probably willing to listen for another thirty seconds. If it's shallow and practically inaudible, the person is probably wondering why he ever answered the phone and how he's going to get you off the line. If the answer sounds hurried or distracted, you know that the listener is actively engaged in something more important. If the tone is gruff, you know you've got about five seconds before he ends the call.

When you hear a response like "Fine," say something like, "That's good!" or "Glad to hear it!" Deliver the words in a warm natural way as if you had called your favorite aunt to check on her health. If you seem to care about the decision maker's well-being, you're more likely to be perceived as someone who is truly interested in the company's welfare, not just in making a sale.

## AND YOU?

### Reply simply and sincerely.

Polite people return your greeting: "I'm fine. How are you?"

At this stage you may be thinking, "Why are we wasting all this time with this b.s.? I've got a sales quota to fill." So, instead of politely answering the decision maker's inquiry about your health, you dismiss his question by rapidly saying something like "Fine, fine," and you start selling.

Now you've insulted the person you're trying to impress. He was nice enough to ask about you and, on some level, felt good about himself for being polite, even to a telemarketer. He tried being nice. Now he realizes that you never really cared at all. Don't blow it in the first five seconds of your call.

Some sales folks go too far in answering this polite question with responses like, "If I felt any better, I wouldn't know what I'd do with myself," or "Getting better every day," or "I feel great!"

Instead, answer inquiries about your well-being by saying something like, "I'm doing well. Thanks for asking!" The answer is short (which is what the decision maker wants) and builds trust (accomplished by saying something nice to a stranger).

## VARIATIONS

### Go with the flow.

Of course, things rarely go exactly as planned. Some decision makers will use your greeting as a way to cut you off. Here are a few examples with suggested responses.

Table 6

| *Decision Maker Says:* | *You Say:* |
|---|---|
| *I'm busy. What can I do for you?* | *I understand. I was calling to talk with you about our product that does XYZ. I'll only take a minute.* |
| | |
| *I can't talk with you right now. One of our long-time employees died, and the funeral's today.* | *Oh, I'm so sorry. I'll try to reach you another time. Would that be OK?* |
| | |
| *I'm trying to get over a cold. How can I help you?* | *I'm sorry to hear that. I'll only be a minute.* |
| | |
| *What do you want?!* | *Our product does XYZ, and I wanted to give you a few details. Would you like to hear about it?* |
| | |
| *Who did you say this is?* | *This is Stewart Rogers with ABC Computer. I wanted to tell you briefly about a new product that does XYZ. Would you like to hear about it briefly?* |
| | |
| *If you're selling something, I'm not interested!* | *I am selling something, a product that can help you to XYZ. Would you like to hear about it briefly?* |

## DETRACTORS

### Plead guilty as charged.

I can't finish this chapter without addressing those who believe that asking "How are you?" at the outset of a call is seriously dumb. As an example, I've extracted this quote from Nancy Friedman, who calls herself "the Telephone Doctor."

(available online at http://www.myarticlearchive.com/articles/6/294.htm)

"At Telephone Doctor, we call the phrase, 'Hi, how are you?' the four killer words. They are probably the most useless words you can utter when making cold sales calls—or even warm ones.

"Years ago, while living at our house, my mother answered our phone. After her gentle, 'Hello' came 'Hi, Mrs. Friedman' (she wasn't Mrs. Friedman). 'How are you?'

"My mother, an open, honest person, simply went on to say, 'I'm so glad you asked. My back is killing me, my pacemaker is a little slow, the sore on my knee looks horrible, I've got the worst headache, and feel like I'm getting the flu. How are you?' The man on the phone said, 'Compared to you, a whole lot better,' and hung up.

"The phrase, 'Hi, how are you?' is useless for making sales calls. Don't use it. Opening a call with, 'Hi, how are you,' tells the prospect, 'I'm out to sell you something.'"

I'll quickly address two points about Ms. Friedman's comments. First, she seems to imply that asking about someone's well-being might force you to actually hear the answer. Listening to a prospect is a good thing. In this case, I would have sympathized with her mother's ailments and established myself as a kind, considerate person. No harm there.

Secondly, Ms. Friedman seems concerned that the listener will discover that you're selling something. So what? You *are* selling something. That's the truth. And the prospect already knows it. After all, you're a stranger, which means you're either a salesman or a bill collector. Most folks are relieved I'm the former and not the latter.

If being friendly is a sign of weakness, I plead guilty as charged.

# CHAPTER THIRTY-ONE

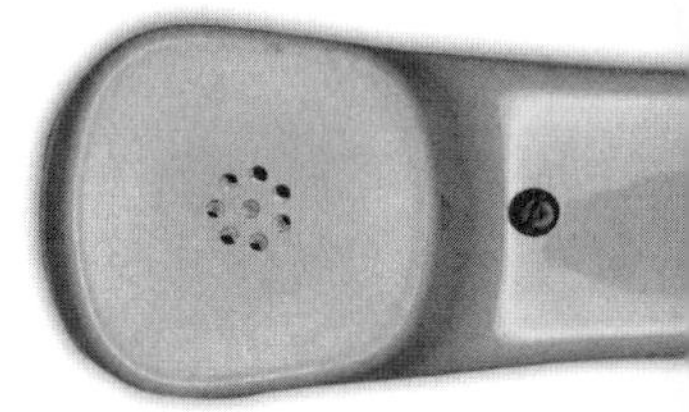

# The fifteen-second introduction

THE OBJECT OF EVERY STEP in the sales process is to move to the next step. After the greeting, introduce yourself and the product.

## ESSENTIAL MESSAGE

### Focus your power.

After the greeting, your next step is to communicate the "essential message" about your product in a way that leads the person to want to hear more.

The "essential message" is a one to two sentence statement describing what your product does and how it will benefit the buyer, delivered in fifteen seconds or less. It is what you want the buyer to remember, even if he forgets everything else.

The key to successful telemarketing is the ability to describe your product and its value in a few words. As the world becomes more complex and attention spans get shorter, simplifying and focusing your message becomes critically important. Think of yourself as a laser beam cutting through the clutter and penetrating deeply and permanently into the buyer's brain. There's no room for elaborate descriptions on this trip, no time to explain every wonderful feature and benefit, or the inner workings of your technological marvel. You only have a few seconds to gain a foothold before the listener moves on.

As Mark Twain said, "If I had more time, I would have written less." After you have studied as much as you can about your product, your first task is to condense your essential message into a few words. As Twain reminds us, that takes time. I've heard that President Eisenhower required his staff to condense their ideas into a single sheet of paper before submitting them to him, contending that longer statements had not been considered carefully enough.

Advertising is the art of conveying the essential message. For example, consider those thousands of TV commercials hyping prescription drugs. The products are highly complex with funny-sounding names that come with reels of fine print. However, the message of these commercials is simple, regardless of the specific drug being advertised: "Take this drug, and you'll have a better life." That's the essential message. In the end, it's the only message that matters. Consumers will forget the technical explanation for the medication and dismiss the potential side effects, but they will remember the essential message for a lifetime.

One more analogy: Imagine that you're on your deathbed with fifteen seconds to live. Your family is gathered around, leaning down to hear your last words as you slip away forever. You want to say something profound, something that will console your loved ones, something so important that they will repeat your last words over and over to future generations. (No pressure, huh?) You have fifteen seconds to say twenty-five words. What would they be?

## SCRIPT

### Grab 'em quick.

Here is a simple example of a fifteen-second introduction that incorporates the essential message.

*Briefly . . .*

*My name is Stewart Rogers. I work for ABC Computer here in Raleigh.*

*We've developed an amazing computer system that can link your offices at half the cost.*

*I'd like to give you a few details about how it works.*

*Would you like to hear about it briefly?*

The purpose of each word and phrase is explained below:

**Table 7**

| You Say: | Purpose: |
|---|---|
| Briefly | The first word out of your mouth reassures the listener that your comments will be brief, that unlike some telemarketers who drone on and on, you will respect the decision maker's valuable time. |
| My name is Stewart Rogers. I work for ABC Computer here in Raleigh. | You repeat your name and your company's name, adding the company location. |
| | |

(Continued on next page)

Table 7 (continued)

| You Say: | Purpose: |
|---|---|
| We've developed an amazing computer system that can link your offices at half the cost. | You describe what you're selling and exactly how it will benefit the decision maker. This is your "essential message." (Include at least one superlative adjective to generate excitement.) |
| | |
| I'd like to give you a few details about how it works. Would you like to hear about it briefly? | You set the agenda for the next step and ask permission to proceed. |

This approach works for three important reasons. First, by condensing your pitch to a few simple words, you enable the listener to immediately understand what you're selling. Second, by asking permission to continue, you show respect for the person's time. And third, by asking for an immediate reaction to your pitch, you gain an honest, unfiltered look at the prospect's gut-level reaction to your offering.

Some sellers would object to asking for a response so early in the conversation, arguing that—without more detail from you—the decision maker is more likely to say "No" than "Yes." I contend that the buyer is more likely to say "No" than "Yes" anyway. My interest in asking is not to solicit a final buying decision, but to get all the cards out on the table as quickly as possible.

For example, if the decision maker indicates that he has absolutely no interest in what I'm selling, then I know that the chances of changing his mind are slim and that my time is better spent making other calls. If the answer is a qualified "No," and the prospect articulates his/her objections, I'll know exactly what problems I'm facing and focus my time and energy on solving them.

A "Maybe" tells me that a seed already exists within the buyer that needs to be nourished—and that the buyer *wants* me to nourish it. A "Yes" means that a seed of interest has already sprouted within the listener and that my job is to understand why the person already has an interest and how I can best develop it.

In all cases, I'm looking for an immediate, visceral reaction to my offering: a spur-of-the-moment, gut-level, unrehearsed, raw impression response, which is the kind of information that consistently predicts sales success.

# CHAPTER THIRTY-TWO

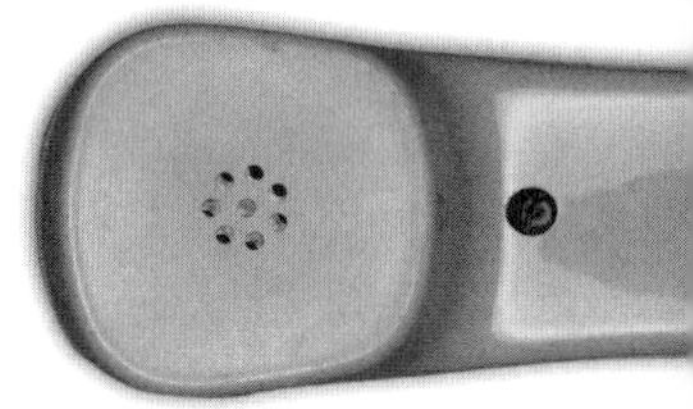

# The sixty-second overview

SURPRISE! SURPRISE! THE DECISION MAKER actually wants to hear more about your product!

In a perfect world, you would stop the clock, take a deep breath, and gather your thoughts. Despite having a long history of making outbound calls, I'm still surprised—and nervous—when a prospect wants to know more. My first thought is "I have to be perfect. This is a chance of a lifetime. I may never gain this person's undivided attention again."

In reality, 99.9 percent of us would be unemployed if our jobs depended on a perfect performance every time. Plus, I've found that a buyer who demands perfection is probably not a customer you want anyway. We don't have to be perfect; but we do need to be good, very good, to succeed in the high stress world of B2B telemarketing.

Reassure yourself with the knowledge that the decision maker is willing to listen, that the essential message about your product pushed some kind of button inside the person's head. Take solace knowing that you're offering something that the person may actually need, that you're trying to help this person, not pick his pocket.

The decision maker is asking for information because he wants it, not because you've tricked him, or hypnotized him, or bullied him into listening. You're delivering a service. You're doing a good deed. You're trying to help.

Your job at this stage is simply to present the basic details about your product in a concise, professional way, displaying a positive personality and a genuine concern for the buyer. If you're offering something the person wants and can afford, you'll make a sale. If you're not, you won't. It's that simple. Despite tall tales of great salespeople who can sell ice to Eskimos (although I'll bet that some actually need prepackaged ice), you can't convince a business decision maker to buy something he doesn't want. Don't try.

Think of yourself as a tour guide, introducing the decision maker to the wonders of your wizardry. He's looking for answers. You're there to help.

> "It's simple: Sell to people who want your product; ignore those who don't."
>
> —Guy Kawasaki

## SCRIPT

### Hit the highlights.

The sixty-second overview goes like this:

**Table 8**

| | |
|---|---|
| Who | *Again, my name is David Wagoner. I work for Computer Concepts here in Raleigh. We've been in business for the last eight years serving a variety of companies in this area.* |

(Continued on next page)

Table 8 (continued)

| | |
|---|---|
| What | *We've developed a unique system for networking multiple offices that allows more data to be shared at a lower cost. The system uses patented technology working with your existing hardware to increase the efficiency of your data transmissions and reduce your communication expenses.*<br>*The features of our technology include:*<br>*1. A high-speed KVM switching system that enables you to manage multiple servers from a single location;*<br>*2. A transmission optimizer to ensure that your priority data is always sent in the most economical manner; and*<br>*3. Proactive monitoring of IT operations so that staff can fix problems before they hinder service levels.* |
| Why | *That simply means that your staff can get the information they need, when they need it, at a lower cost to you.* |
| When | *At this time, we're offering a sixty-day free trial to all of our new customers.* |
| Excitement | *We're excited about our product and wanted to let you know about it.* |
| Transitional Question | *Do you think it might be of some help to you?* |

## TRANSITIONAL QUESTIONS

### Pass the baton.

At the end of your sixty-second presentation you want to ask a question that gets the prospect talking. To that point, you've been doing all the gabbing. If you don't transition this monologue into a discussion, you can't move forward.

Telemarketers who employ the "dark side of the Force" use the "death-by-talking" technique. Once they get started, they never stop until you're so tired of listening that you'll agree to anything. They don't ask questions, because they're not interested in any answer except "yes."

Another infamous technique used by the Darth Vader School of Telemarketing is to ask rhetorical questions following a monologue. These are designed to manipulate, rather than gain information. As a result they insult the intelligence of the listener and destroy any hope of trust between the parties. A classic example is, "Would you like to save money?" followed immediately by a snappy retort like "Then you'll love our product."

Ask questions in order to understand the listener, not to manipulate him/her. After your initial monologue, open a conversation as soon as possible by asking an open-ended, transitional question like the one shown above, "Do you think this might be of some help to you?"

Here's why each word is important:

**Table 9**

| Word/Phrase | Why It Works Best |
|---|---|
| Do you think . . . | You could say: "How do you feel about the product?" I've found that asking what a stranger thinks is better than asking what he feels, even though the person's emotional reaction to your offering is ultimately more important than his logical assessment. Asking someone's feeling implies a certain level of intimacy which you have not established. Asking about feelings is threatening. Asking about opinions is not. |

(Continued on next page)

**Table 9** (continued)

| | |
|---|---|
| Do you think it might be . . . | I could ask: "Do you think this product would be of some help?" Using this verb forces the prospect to give an up or down vote on your product at that moment. Considering that you've only been on the phone for seventy-five seconds, it's too early to ask a prospect to make a final decision, particularly if the product is complex, expensive, and so on. All you want to do is get the person to recognize and say that the product "might" be helpful. This moves the person one step closer to a purchase in a nonthreatening way. |
| Do you think it might be of some help . . . | Using the qualifier "some" is another way to make it easier for the prospect to move forward. In the dating world, you might say: "Do you want to go out to dinner sometime?" The word "some" implies that the date doesn't have to be today or necessarily any time soon, just at some time in the future. That essentially rephrases the question to: "Would you ever be willing to go out with me?" If the answer is "no," then you know you're out of luck. If it's "yes," you're making progress. The object of selling is to make progress, even slowly if necessary, toward your ultimate goal. |

(Continued on next page)

Table 9 (continued)

| | |
|---|---|
| Do you think it might be of some help to you? | Finally, the best questions use the word "you," a personal sounding pronoun that implies a personal concern for the person to whom you're speaking. You could say, "Do you think this would be of any help to your company?" Replacing "you" with "your company" would remove the one-to-one connection and force the prospect to speak for the best interests of the company as a whole. Remember that people buy things. Companies don't. Decision makers may technically represent the enterprise, but they are naturally concerned about their own day-to-day problems. They're more likely to think something benefiting them also benefits the company than something benefiting the company necessarily benefits them as individuals. |

By now you've greeted the decision maker, introduced the product, and delivered a sixty-second introduction ending with a transitional question. Your next move depends on the decision maker's response.

## WHAT'S NEXT?

### Turn right at the crossroads.

At this point, the listener will have one of the following responses, discussed in detail in the next five chapters:

*Yes: Sign me up.*

*Maybe: Answer my question.*

*Maybe: Ask me a question.*

*Maybe: I have objections.*

*No: I'm not interested.*

# CHAPTER THIRTY-THREE

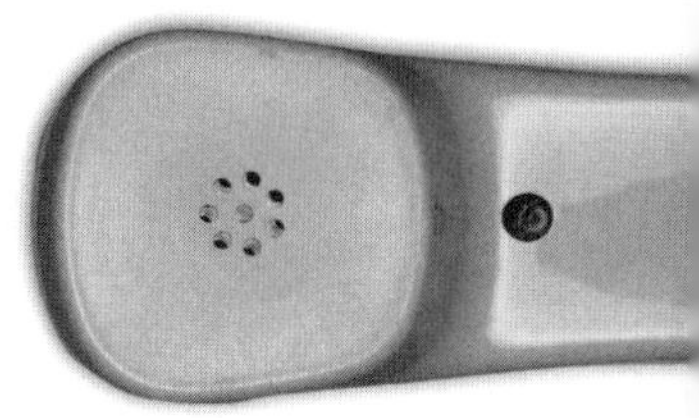

# "Yes!"

In telemarketing heaven, everybody you call wants to buy what you're selling . . . right now, at full price. Oh happy day! Peace on earth! Good will to sales folks!

The cool part is that even though this happens rarely, it still happens. If you're selling the right product to the right people at the right time at the right price, you'll get some winners!

Sometimes they'll interrupt what you're saying and ask, "Where do I sign?" or "When can you deliver it?" or "Do you take credit cards?" They see your vision. They share your excitement. They can't wait to pay you.

## CALL TO ACTION

### Find the courage to ask.

While some decision makers voluntarily agree to your proposition without being asked, most need a "call to action": a request to take the next step. Depending on your objective, you might ask someone to make a direct purchase, participate in a product demonstration, meet with an outside sales rep, or receive product information.

Many sales folks feel uncomfortable about making such a request. They're fine introducing themselves, explaining their products, answering questions, and even responding to objections. But when the conversation is over and the moment arrives to take the next step, they're speechless. Like the guy at the bar who charms a new woman for thirty minutes, but can't quite get himself to ask for her phone number, the telemarketer who can't ask for action is going home alone.

## TIMING

### Recognize the right moment.

The Cialis commercials on TV crack me up! They always feature this poor guy who has to spend all day waiting for his woman to get in the mood. Luckily, his erectile dysfunction pills work for thirty-six hours so that he'll be ready when she is. The slogan says it all: "Will you be ready when the time is right?"

That's a reasonable question in sales. Will you be ready when the customer is ready to say "Yes"?

Here are a few clues that indicate it's time to pop the question.

*Praise*—The decision maker is praising your product, explaining why it's exactly the solution he needs, detailing the good things he's heard about it from others, and saying that now is the right time to buy.

*All the right answers*—You're asking the buyer concluding questions that are being answered positively without exception:

You: *So, do you like the new features?*

Dec mkr: *Yes.*

You: *Do you think this will work OK with your existing system?*

Dec mkr: *Yes.*

You: *Do you have a budget for it this year?*

Dec mkr: *Yes.*

(Kiss her, you fool! It's like a soap opera where the hero stares into the heroine's eyes, asking her increasingly more seductive questions until, at last, their lips smash together.)

*Problem solved*—You and the decision maker have been examining a potential problem related to your product, a technical issue, or a question about an important feature. After extensive research, the two of you have reached a mutual agreement that your gizmo will do what he wants it to do. You're both relieved. Act now while everybody's happy. Ask for the sale.

*The long pause*—You summarize what you and the decision maker have been saying all along: your product is the right solution at the right time. You end your comments with a powerful closing statement and stop talking. One, two, three, four, five seconds tick by. You're waiting for the buyer to say something. He doesn't. You ask for the sale.

## THE MAGIC WORDS

### Ask in the right way.

Let's start with a few ways you shouldn't ask for a sale, such as asking the person whether he or she wants to buy what you're selling. It's OK for the clerk in the dollar store to ask whether you want to buy the handful of items you've scooped up walking down the aisles. But it's not OK to use that word when talking to a businessperson.

First, the man/woman who's making the buying decision may not be the one actually writing the check. So the decision maker would prefer to think of himself/herself as an "authorizing agent" rather than a buyer. And even if the buyer and the check writer are one and the same, business owners like to think of themselves as superior to common folks, more suited to making investments than handling grubby old dollars.

Another mistake in asking for the sale is to be cute about it, saying something such as, "How would you like to pay for this?" or "Do you want the deluxe model or the regular model?" before the person has actually agreed to buy the product in the first place. For the wheeler-dealers of the world, this kind of trickery is designed to avoid a yes or no answer, and get the cash out of the buyer's pocket before he knows what's happening. This kind of slight-of-hand may work selling secondhand aluminum siding, but it's a red flag for most business decision makers, who may be willing to buy, but won't be pushed into it.

As with other techniques in successful telemarketing, I recommend the low-key, straightforward approach, using questions such as:

*Is this something you'd like to do?*

*Would you like to move forward with this?*

*Would you like for me to go ahead and ship it to you?*

If your objective is something other than a direct sale, your "call to action" might be one of the following:

Table 10

| Objective | Call to Action |
|---|---|
| Literature | Would you like to receive written information? I'd like to send a brochure to you. Is that OK with you? |

(Continued on next page)

**Table 10** (continued)

| | |
|---|---|
| Call Back | When do you want me to call you back?<br>I'll call you on Friday. Is that OK? |
| Proposal | Would you be interested in receiving a detailed proposal?<br>I'd like to prepare a detailed proposal for you. Is that OK? |
| Meeting | Would you be willing to meet with one of our sales representatives to discuss the details?<br>When would be a convenient time? |

# CHAPTER THIRTY-FOUR

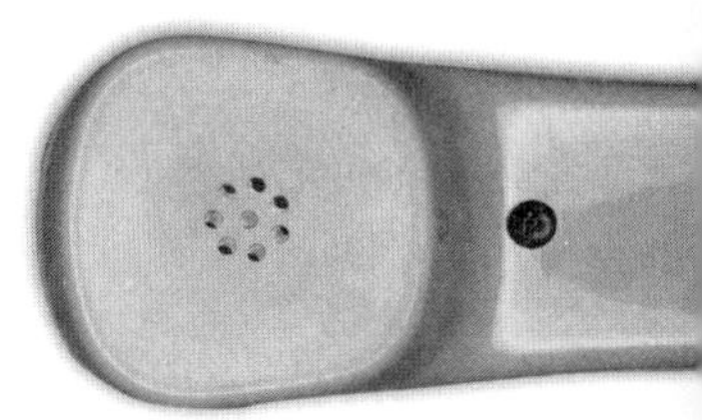

## "I have a question."

ALMOST AS VALUABLE AS PROSPECTS who say yes are those who ask questions. In fact, I have found that a substantial percentage of decision makers who immediately agree with your pitch are impulse buyers, who don't experience the roller-coaster, mind-body reconciliation until much farther down the sales cycle. These are the folks who order the product, but return it unopened.

People who ask questions are actually thinking about your product in an immediate and practical way. They are trying to visualize your solution and try it on for size. They are anticipating implementation barriers and operational limitations. They are imagining all the headaches they will lose, and all the benefits they will reap.

A person who asks questions is usually trying to remove objections, not prove them. He wants to buy and wants your help to accomplish that goal. Like a moviegoer who leaves his everyday concerns at the door and plunges into the images on the screen, the person who asks substantive questions about a new product to a stranger on the phone is looking for a happy ending. Help him find one!

Pay attention to the first question (or comment) out of the prospect's mouth. It's probably the most important one. Answer this one to the prospect's satisfaction and he'll be ready to talk turkey. Miss this one, and feel the door slam as you walk out.

## THANKS

### Reinforce their interest.

Before you start answering a question, give thanks for it. Tell the person that you appreciate the time and effort he's spending with you. "Thanks for taking the time to discuss this question with me."

The weak and the manipulative hate questions, because they're afraid that the truth will expose them for who they are. Strong, ethical sellers have nothing to fear. They welcome questions. They believe that the more a prospect knows about a product, the more likely the person is to sell it.

Buyers know this too. Subconsciously, they're judging your reaction to being asked a question, just as carefully as the answer you deliver. If you're afraid of questions, they're afraid of you and what you're selling. Fearful folks don't buy. They run.

## THE REAL ISSUE

### Get to the heart of the matter.

You can't answer a question unless you understand what it really means. If your wife asks you if you find another woman attractive, she could be asking lots of things that have nothing to do with the specific female in question—such as whether you find her attractive. If your boss asks whether you feel overworked, he could be truly interested, or he could be asking why you haven't accomplished what he wanted you to accomplish.

Questions from decision makers work the same way. Intentionally or not, the question asked may not specifically indicate what he wants to know. The successful telemarketer not only understands the real question behind the question, but also knows what answer the questioner wants to hear.

For example, a decision maker who wants to know whether your company is trustworthy and competent might ask questions like:

- *Who's your largest customer?*
- *How long has your company been in business?*
- *How many people work for your company?*
- *Is your company going to be represented at the (big time association) trade show this year?*

## ACTIVE LISTENING

### Reflect what you hear.

Active listening is an effective way to understand the real meaning behind a question or a statement made by a decision maker. Essentially, the technique involves listening to the actual spoken words, interpreting the true meaning behind them, and then restating this interpretation back to the speaker.

For example, if the VIP asks, "How many people work for your company?" you might respond by answering the question directly, and then illuminating the bigger question behind the question:

Dec mkr: *How many people work for your company?*

You: *We have about eighty staff working here at our corporate headquarters.*

*Are you concerned that our company might be too small to provide the quality and customer service you need?*

Active listening also works in interpreting statements. For example:

Dec mkr: *We tried this once before and could never get the thing to work. The company that sold it to us promised to have it working in thirty days. Their technicians spent a week here and then never came back.*

You: *I'm sorry to hear that. Are you concerned that this will happen to you again?*

Some would disagree with this approach, contending that the hidden objection is best left hidden, that shedding light on a vague concern in someone's mind only makes a mountain out of a mole hill. Among these detractors are timid souls who are afraid to look at the truth and simply hope it will disappear as the sales process progresses. Others are manipulators who fear being exposed by the truth and use fast talk to skirt past it.

My contention is that honesty is the foundation upon which successful selling is built, not only from an ethical perspective, but also from a practical one. You can spend all day explaining the superiority of your product, only to lose the sale because of an unspoken objection that you were unable, or unwilling, to identify and tackle.

## WHAT THEY WANT TO HEAR

### Be honest in the most positive way.

For every question asked, there is an answer that the person wants to hear.

"Telling the customer what he wants to hear" can be ethical or criminal, depending on your interpretation. Rip-off artists, for example, simply lie about features and benefits to fulfill the consumer's expectations. "Got cancer? Our elixir cures cancer. Need oil for your car? Our potion does that too." The power of a sleazy salesperson is in knowing exactly what the potential buyer wants to hear, and then saying it without regard to the truth.

Ironically, an ethical salesperson's power also derives from knowing what a decision maker wants to hear. The difference is that the straight shooter tells the truth, but tells it in the most favorable terms. For example, if a buyer asks whether a particular machine can produce one hundred widgets an hour, both the honest and the dishonest seller know that the buyer wants to hear, "Yes." The sleaze-ball answers, "Yes," knowing that actual production is half that. The honest telemarketer says, "No. Our technology produces fifty widgets an hour, but with 25 percent less waste."

The examples below illustrate typical questions and effective responses:

**Table 11**

| Concern | Question Asked | What Buyer Wants to Hear | Sample Answer |
|---|---|---|---|
| Features | Does your product have that new XYZ turbocharger I've been hearing about? | You can accomplish more in less time. | We offer something better called ABC Booster that operates more efficiently than any accelerator product on the market! |
| Benefits | How long will it take for us to recover our cost on the investment? | You can recover your costs in a short time. | The typical return-on-investment for a facility of your size is two years which is the best ROI in the industry! |

(Continued on next page)

**Table 11** (continued)

| | | | |
|---|---|---|---|
| Service | How long will it take to implement your solution? | You can start using it without delay. | Based on our extensive experience with facilities like yours, we can implement our software in eight to ten weeks. Nobody can match us for service before and after the sale! |
| Price | Is there a discount for bulk purchases? | You can get a good price. | Absolutely! You can save 20 percent on our economy package. |

# CHAPTER THIRTY-FIVE

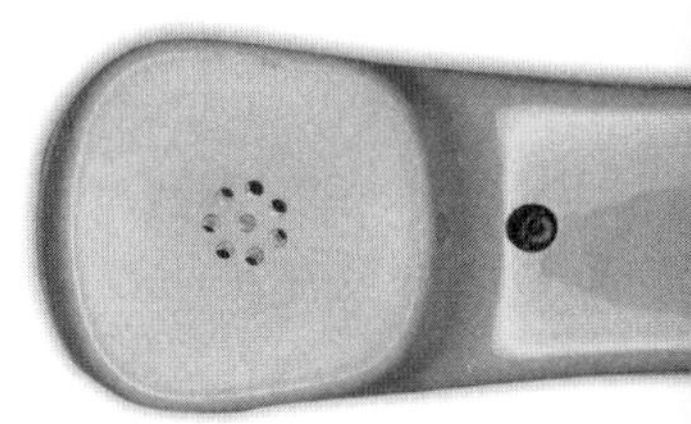

# "Ask me a question."

After you deliver the sixty-second overview and ask the decision maker whether he or she is interested in your product, you may not get a definite answer. The person doesn't say yes, but he doesn't say no, indicating that (1) he's so bedazzled by your presentation that he's speechless, (2) he has no authority, or (3) he's giving serious thought to your proposition.

Concentrate on the third possibility and begin asking questions in order to better understand the individual's sense of need, and to what degree your product may fill that need.

## BASICS

### Choose the right tool.

*Information gathering questions*—The best use of a question is the most common one—gathering information. "How many servers do you have? Where are they located? What operating systems are they using?" The more you know about the decision maker's situation, the better job you'll do in matching your product to the person's needs.

*Directional questions*—These inquiries are designed to direct the conversation in a particular way. "Have you considered an environmentally friendly roofing alternative?" "Are you aware that leasing is often more economical than buying?" These kind of questions allow you to switch the subject, or add another building block to your sales presentation.

While the purpose of the question is to redirect the conversation, the tone should be nonmanipulative. For example, a hard-driving, close-at-all-costs seller might ask the two questions above in a more intimidating way such as, "Do you want to keep damaging the environment or do something worthwhile for future generations?" or "Do you want to keep wasting money or lease instead?" The object of a directional question is to persuade the driver that turning the corner voluntarily is in his best interest, not to bully the guy into following your directions.

*Confirming questions*—Questions can be helpful in summarizing what a decision maker has just said. For example, if the person has been discussing how competitive products have failed to integrate easily with existing systems, how sales reps often promise more than they deliver, and how the final price is usually more than the original quote, you might ask: "Then you're looking for a product that works seamlessly with your existing systems at a reliable price. Is that correct?" This technique is also an example of active listening.

## DON'T

### Be careful what you ask.

*Don't ask a question if you already know the answer.* They say that good lawyers always know the answers before they question witnesses. That technique may work well for Perry

Mason, but asking a decision maker to repeat what you already know is a waste of time, and usually perceived as tedious and manipulative by the listener. As previously explained, confirming questions can be valuable, but only when new information has come forth in an actual conversation. There's no point in asking the CFO if he's the CFO, or in asking whether his plant manufactures textiles when you already know it does.

Instead, use what you know to ask a related question. For example, let's say that you've researched a manufacturer on the Internet and learned that the company was recently cited by OSHA for safety violations ... and you just happen to be selling educational materials related to OSHA compliance. You could call the plant's safety director and say, "I hear you've been charged by OSHA. Is that true?" Or you could say, "Would you be interested in a complete set of OSHA regulations and training materials?" The first approach reminds the decision maker of his failures and public humiliation. The second says, "I'm on your side. We don't have to talk about your unfortunate past. Let me help you make things better in the future!"

*Don't ask stupid questions*—We've all heard questions from TV interviewers that are just plain stupid, such as asking an Academy Award nominee, "How excited are you to be nominated for best actress?" or asking a defeated candidate, "How disappointed are you by the outcome?" For some strange reason, interviewers must think that these questions are more intelligent than simply asking, "Are you excited?" or "Are you disappointed?" They're all stupid questions. Everyone knows the answers.

Stupid business questions include: "Do you want to save money?" or "Do you want to double your income?" Only a suicidal decision maker would answer no. These kinds of questions generate no meaningful information and do nothing to guide the conversation toward a successful outcome. They only send a message to the VIP that you're either manipulative or dumb, neither of which are exactly glowing recommendations.

*Don't ask threatening questions*—Certain information about the decision maker and his/her company is private and confidential and, therefore, unavailable to telemarketers. Ironically, in order to be a successful seller, you need to know the buyer's bottom line problems in order to best position your wares. But at the same time, asking a question that crosses the confidentiality threshold will have the opposite effect. You'll be perceived as a threat, closing the door to any future sales opportunity.

## STEP-BY-STEP

### Take it slow.

The trick is to ask questions that dig for real answers, but are not intimidating to the person being asked. For example, consider the subtle differences in these two questions: "Has your computer network gone down recently?" versus "Are computer outages a problem for you?"

Question one sounds like something you'd be asked on the witness stand. "What happened? When did it happen? Why did it happen?" The decision maker is being asked to confess to a problem. Question two is more general and less threatening. Both questions are designed to lead toward a discussion of system outages and how your network management solution can minimize those problems. Question two is much more likely to succeed.

As in personal relationships, sharing private information in business relationships happens over time. The more the buyer trusts you, the more likely he or she is to volunteer inside information. Of course, you're never going to find out who's pilfering office supplies or sleeping with the receptionist, but you may discover the practical problems that keep the VIP from sleeping at night.

While some decision makers may never share their real problems with a salesperson, or even with their fellow employees, many want to solve what's bugging them. They want to confide in someone who is trustworthy and capable of removing the stones in their shoes. That someone can be you.

If the buyer hints at a problem, ask follow-up questions. For example, the conversation might go something like this:

Buyer: *Some aspects of our manufacturing process are just too expensive.*

You: *Really? What's an example?*

Buyer: *Well, like packaging the final product.*

You: *How are you doing that now?*

Buyer: *It's mostly hands-on now, which is OK, but there are always lots of mistakes, stoppages in the production line, things like that. I wish there was a more automated way of handling it that we could afford.*

You: *How many units are you turning out now, say in an hour?*

Buyer: *Our goal is 1,000. But the average is probably 750.*

Now you've gotten to the heart of the matter. The buyer needs an affordable, automated packaging system that produces at least 1,000 units an hour. Now you have the critical information you need to pitch your solution.

## CONCLUSIONS

### Wrap it up in a nice package.

After ten to fifteen minutes of questions and answers, summarize what you've heard in a positive way, and ask for confirmation. For example:

*Thanks for talking with me about your situation!*

*From what I understand, you are a contract manufacturer who focuses on the auto aftermarket with customers throughout the Southeast. Your average production is 750 units per hour, but you'd like to increase that to 1,000. And you believe you can do that by automating your packaging.*

*Is that an accurate description?*

After the decision maker OKs your description or amends it, move on to the role that your product can play in the process:

*Our product would be perfect for your environment. Here's why… .*

# CHAPTER THIRTY-SIX

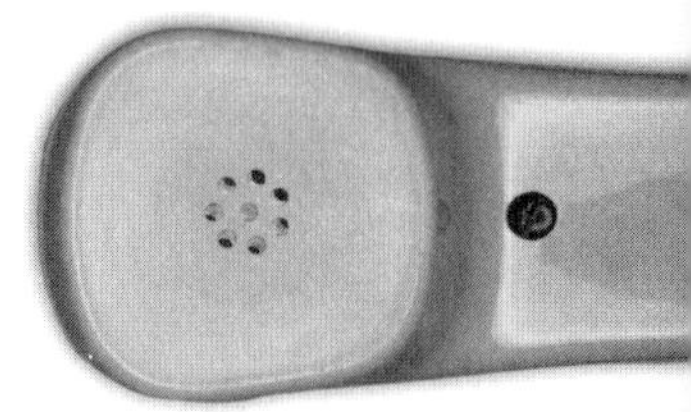

## "I have an objection."

THE UNFORTUNATE TRUTH IS THAT most decision makers will respond to your sixty-second introduction with an objection.

Objections come in all shapes and sizes. They may be big or small, real or imagined, easily fixable or impossible to overcome. They may relate to you, your company, or your product. They may concern features or benefits and arise from logical or emotional concerns.

To the pessimistic seller, an objection is a reason *not* to buy. To the optimist it's the key to closing the sale. For example, if the buyer says, "Your product is too expensive," the person is really saying, "I'll buy this if the price is right." By knowing that the price is the key to the sale, you know that you must somehow find a price—or a payment plan—that is acceptable to the buyer. Maybe you'll offer a discount. Maybe you'll explain why your price is reasonable, considering the pricing of comparable products. Maybe you'll reemphasize the product's value. Maybe you'll talk about return-on-investment (ROI).

A successful telemarketer is a mind reader of sorts, processing every word, every sound, and every pause instantaneously, in order to gain a clear view of the buyer's thoughts and emotions. The more you know, the more likely you are to close the deal. By voicing an objection, the buyer tells you what matters most. Overcome that barrier, relieve that anxiety, answer that question, and you'll be cruising carefree down Sales Boulevard.

## BEFORE YOU START

### Thank the doubter.

Before we discuss specific types of objections and how to respond to them, remember to thank the person for sharing information with you, before you try to convince him to do something different. Try something like, "Oh, thanks for letting me know."

After all, he's making your job easier by telling you facts you didn't know already.

And reverse psychology often works. Do the unexpected, and he might respond unexpectedly. Show him that you're a nice guy, and he may be a nicer guy in return. He's expecting an argument. Give him an agreement.

## NO NEED

### Help without criticizing.

This objection typically means one of three things:

*The buyer doesn't have the problem your product is designed to fix.*

You're selling software that protects PCs against Internet hackers, and you call someone who doesn't own a computer. Oops .... You're going to have a tough time convincing this person to buy a solution for a problem he's never experienced and won't be experiencing any time in the immediate future. As the song goes, "Here's a quarter. Call somebody who cares."

*The buyer has the problem, but doesn't recognize or acknowledge it.*

You're selling security software to a computer owner whose PC has never been invaded by a virus and sees no need to protect himself against an attack he's never endured. In this case, your job, like that of an insurance agent, is to convince the buyer that, even though he doesn't need your product now, he will need it some day soon.

Another example: you're selling office furniture. You pitch your nifty-jiffy simulated wood executive desks to a decision maker who immediately says, "We don't need any more desks!"

Instead of wimping away, you respond, "How are they holding up?" The buyer answers "Fine," without hesitation, but then, after a few seconds, adds, "Well, some of those desks *are* pretty old and worn out. Maybe we need to replace a few of them."

*The buyer already has a solution for that problem and doesn't see a need to change.*

The more likely example of the "need" objection occurs when the buyer has already solved the problem you're offering to solve, or at least thinks he has. You'll hear, "We're already using something else." "Someone already handles that for us." In this case, the decision maker recognizes the problem, but believes he already has a solution.

Ask a few questions to better understand the situation.

- *What do you like best about your current solution?*
- *Is your current solution able to do X or Y? (features offered by your product, but not by the competitor's)*
- *If you could design your own solution, what would it do?*

Your temptation is to convince the person who doesn't see a need that he's wrong, that he's too stupid to recognize the problem, or too stupid to know that his current solution is a disaster. Neither approach is going to get you very far.

The better approach is the "changing world" solution. In this strategy, you educate the person who doesn't recognize a problem that, in these days and times, many other companies like his are already experiencing. You congratulate the backward-looking thinker on his good fortune in having escaped this problem in the past, and extend your hope that his good luck will continue. You don't try to scare him, but simply let him know that you're offering a solution that, in today's environment, is worthy of consideration. Likewise, you congratulate the person with an inadequate solution, for having the foresight to have a solution at all and suggest that it might be time to see what else is on the market.

## NO MONEY

### Find a way.

"If wishes were horses, beggars would ride," they say. Money, or more accurately the lack of it, is always a major objection. It's important, however, to fully understand the problem before trying to solve it.

*Poor*—Some companies simply have no money to spend on your product ... not today, not tomorrow, and probably not next year. They're struggling to keep the lights on. They owe back taxes. They're being sued for bad bills. They're on the verge of bankruptcy. They're experiencing pay cuts, layoffs, and service reductions. Forget it. Wish them well, and move on.

*Cash poor*—These companies are profitable (or at least well financed), but can't afford to outlay any significant amount of cash for a new purchase. Offer payment terms or a subscription model.

*Bargain buyers*—These organizations are always looking for the lowest price on everything. They may not be able, or willing, to pay for a BMW, but they will buy a Kia. The issue is not the allocation of funds per se, but the price.

*Budgeters*—Most organizations develop annual budgets. Major expenditures are typically debated and determined in the last quarter of the preceding fiscal year. Something that is too expensive now may be affordable later.

*Overwhelmed/underfunded*—These companies and institutions have substantial budgets, but experience a crush of competing priorities for these dollars, year after year. In order to execute a sale, you may need either an advocate within the organization who can push your agenda, or a product whose benefits are so significant that they outshine less worthy competitors. Another approach is to arrange a payment plan or subscription model, so that your product can be classified as an operating expense (requiring less budgetary scrutiny), rather than a capital expenditure (where competition for sparse dollars is often greater).

When the decision maker says that he or she can't afford what you're selling, ask a few questions to better understand which of the above categories best fits the situation. For example:

*Is this something that you might be able to do later in the year?*

*Does this fit into your priorities?*

*Have you set a budget for this type of product?*

*Would it help to spread the payments out over time?*

*If we could offer a discount, would that help?*

## NO TIME

### Make it easy.

A common objection is that the company doesn't have the time and resources to implement or use your product now. They're in the middle of a big project, buying another company, moving their offices, replacing the CEO, fixing a major problem, and so on.

Sometimes this objection can be overcome by explaining how simple your product is to install, how your people will train their staff to use it, or how taking the time now will save time later. If the problem is truly a logistical one, this response may work. But in many cases the real problem is that the decision maker is "up to his eyeballs in alligators," and doesn't want to think about anything right now.

Overcoming this objection can be difficult. If the VIP talks about a specific priority that is demanding his attention, ask when that project will be finished. If the completion date is relatively soon, try to close your deal soon thereafter. More often, the current priority has no end date in sight; or the decision maker is always under the gun for something. From the decision maker's perspective, there will never be a good time to do what you're proposing.

In this case, there are four strategies that might work:

*Enhance other priorities.*—If your product will make it easier or cheaper for the decision maker to implement his other priorities, he may be willing to buy sooner. For example, buying a new computer system might make it easier to install a new telephone system.

*Get a quick win.*—Sometimes managers who are making sweeping changes that inconvenience a significant portion of an organization for an extended period, will be interested in a "quick win" to boost morale in the short term. For example, in selling hospital software, I often heard CIOs say that they were too busy to buy our application, because they were implementing a major system overhaul that was also aggravating many of the physicians in the hospital. Our firm was occasionally successful in convincing the CIO that implementing our doctor-friendly software in eight weeks would be a good PR move for the IT Department.

*Satisfy someone important*—Powerful leaders can reorder priorities within an organization. Find someone with significant prestige and passion for your product to champion your case.

*Discount the price*—Retailers move much of their merchandise by offering it at "sale" prices during a limited time. While this technique may work in selling lower priced, commodity-type items, it's a risky approach when selling high-end items. For example, let's say that you offer a 15 percent discount for the purchase of a $50,000 product by the end of a given quarter. In my experience this strategy rarely works. A more likely outcome is that the decision maker misses the deadline, and then insists on receiving the discounted price whenever he decides to buy. As a seller, you're faced with an untenable problem. You can refuse to honor the discount, and probably lose the sale; or you can sell the item at the discounted price, removing any credibility in your future pricing offers. Either way, you lose.

## NO TRUST

### Get back to the basics.

A central theme of this book is that people buy from people they trust. If the buyer doesn't trust you, your company, or your product, the show's over. No deposit. No return.

So how do you know when the issue is trust? Hearing these kinds of comments will give you a clue:

*We'd rather work with a local company.*

*I've heard some negative things about your product.*

*We need to know that you'll stand by your product.*

*You said one thing six months ago, and now you're saying something else. I don't know what to believe.*

*We're looking for a company with experience in our industry.*

*I don't know any of your references.*

When someone questions your credibility, your honesty, or your general trustworthiness, you're likely to get nervous, angry, or both. That's exactly the kind of response that questioning decision makers are looking for in order to confirm their suspicions. Keep your voice calm. Speak in short, sensible sentences. Exhibit an attitude that you want to understand the customer's concern first, before trying to rebut it. Ask clarifying questions:

Dec mkr: *We'd rather work with a local company.*

You: *Are you concerned about our ability to respond to your needs?*

Dec mkr: *I've heard some negative things about your product.*

You: *I'm sorry to hear that! Can you tell me what you've heard?*

Dec mkr: *We need to know that you'll stand by your product.*

You: *Absolutely! Are you concerned that we won't?*

Dec mkr: *You said one thing six months ago, and now you're saying something else. I don't know what to believe.*

You: *Would you explain what you mean?*

Dec mkr: *We're looking for a company with experience in our industry.*

You: *Are there some unique problems about your industry that you think we should know?*

Once you understand the nature of the mistrust, you must resolve this issue. There's no point in extolling the virtues of your product or offering bargain pricing if the buyer doesn't trust you. If the buyer thinks you're selling trash, you won't be able to give it away.

If the issue concerns false information that the buyer may have obtained from a competitor or elsewhere, present the truth clearly, forcefully, and immediately. If the problem concerns a bad experience that the company may have had with one of your other products in the past, fix that problem without delay before trying to sell something new.

If the mistrust is more generalized, reflecting a decision maker's poor experiences with firms or products similar to yours, make it clear that you're different. Construct a "no risk" approach that satisfies the person's misgivings, and shows that your company and its products are more reliable than your competitors.

## NO AUTHORITY

### Deal with decision makers.

Nothing irritates me quite as much as having a long discussion with someone, only to discover that he or she has no purchasing authority. I don't mind if the person is a significant influencer or even a direct analyst. It's the jokers who talk, ask questions, request literature—only to admit that, in the end, they have nothing to do with the outcome—that really bug me!

If you're not sure of a person's role in the buying process, ask:

*Are you the person who would be making a buying decision about this?*

*What role will you play in making the final decision?*

# CHAPTER THIRTY-SEVEN

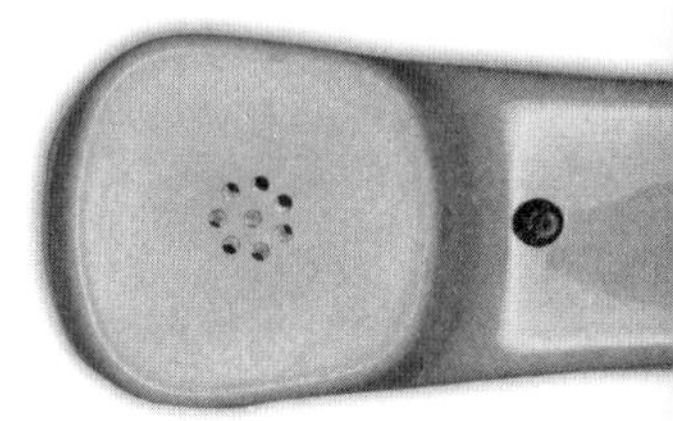

# "I'm not interested."

APPROXIMATELY ONE-THIRD OF THE people I reach by phone say that they're simply "not interested" in my product. They don't explain or articulate an objection. They just say "No!"

When this happens, I typically ask: "Do you have any particular concerns about what I'm selling?" or "Are you experiencing XYZ problem (which my product is designed to fix)?" Their answer is short and not so sweet, "No. I'm not interested. Thank you." And they hang up while I'm formulating the next question. Do not pass Go. Do not collect $200.

What can you do? Not much.

Try to remember that an efficient telemarketer not only identifies interested prospects, but just as importantly, eliminates disinterested ones. If you have a call list of one hundred and, after your first round of calling, can delete fifteen who are absolutely not interested in what you're selling—not today, not tomorrow, not ever—then you've increased the odds of finding interested folks on your next round of calls. Initially, your chances on each call were 1 in 100. Then they improved to 1 in 85.

Sometimes, "No" means no. Make the best of it.

# CHAPTER THIRTY-EIGHT

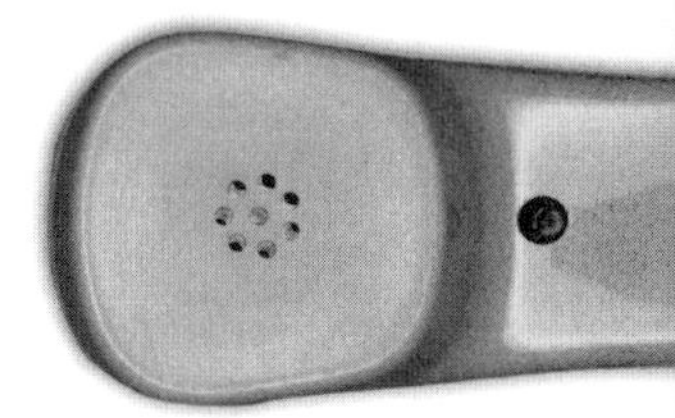

## Leave a message

In the vast majority of your calls to decision makers, you'll reach voice mail. Leave a message. Unlike years past, when secretaries controlled VIP access and personally took all the messages, most of today's executives have direct telephone numbers and review their own voice-mail messages.

### SCRIPT

#### Keep it short and sweet.

An effective voice-mail message is illustrated below:

*Mr. Big, this is David Wagoner.*

*I'm with a company called Computer Concepts here in Atlanta.*

*I'm calling about our amazing new networking device that can cut your system downtime in half.*

*If you would like to hear more about it, please call me.*

*Again, my name is David Wagoner.*

*My phone number is 677-1212.*

*I look forward to hearing from you soon!*

Reflect the same energy and enthusiasm in your voice-mail messages that you do in actual conversation.

If you have a choice between leaving a message with an individual, or leaving one on voice mail, always pick the latter. A human being is more likely to make errors in recording your message, and less likely to actually give the message to the appropriate person. If your only choice is to leave a message with a person, use this basic script:

*My name is Steve Young.*

*My company is Apex Training Services.*

*My phone number is 555-786-8493.*

*I'm calling about our training classes for new real estate agents.*

"Phone tag" is an unavoidable fact in modern business. To reduce missed connections, you can: (1) suggest a specific call-back time when you will be available, (2) ask your colleagues to screen incoming calls and notify you if a particularly hard-to-reach caller is holding, and (3) return calls as quickly as possible.

## WHY MESSAGES MAKES SENSE

### Do the math.

Some people believe that leaving voice-mail messages is a waste of time. After all, they point out, executives hardly ever call back, so the time spent on leaving a message could be better spent on calling someone else who might answer the phone.

I disagree with that assessment. In my experience, not leaving messages is more wasteful than leaving them. Remember that by the time you hear the VIP's voice-mail greeting, you have already expended a significant amount of time in making the call. That includes selecting the record in your database, dialing the number, listening to it ring, and maneuvering past a gatekeeper or voice-mail system. On average, this process takes a minute. That minute is an unavoidable, fixed cost.

So do you write off the expense as a total loss, or do you try to recover the cost? Do you "throw good money after bad" by spending more time leaving a message, or do you just cut your losses?

The key question, of course, is what is to be gained by leaving a message? First, the decision maker might call you back. Yes, it does happen, but only 2–3 percent of the time. From my perspective, even that small of a return-on-investment makes sense. For example, if you make one hundred calls without leaving messages, you expend one hundred minutes with zero return. By contrast, if you leave one hundred messages (at thirty seconds per message), you expend 150 minutes with a 2–3 percent return.

Now if you're selling $2 items by phone, that 2–3 percent return is insignificant. But if you're selling $250,000 software as I've done, 2–3 percent can be a goldmine.

A secondary benefit is less tangible, but still important. By leaving a message you're creating brand awareness, name recognition, or whatever term you use to describe someone remembering you, even if only vaguely. Billions of advertising dollars are spent every year for this purpose. From my perspective I'm more interested in whether the decision maker will recognize my name and company when I call again. When he sees my incoming call on caller-ID, will he pick up the phone and talk with me, or let his voice mail get it? When he does speak to me, will he think that I'm familiar somehow, or a total stranger?

When measured in returned calls and name recognition, voice-mail messages make good sense.

## CHAPTER THIRTY-NINE

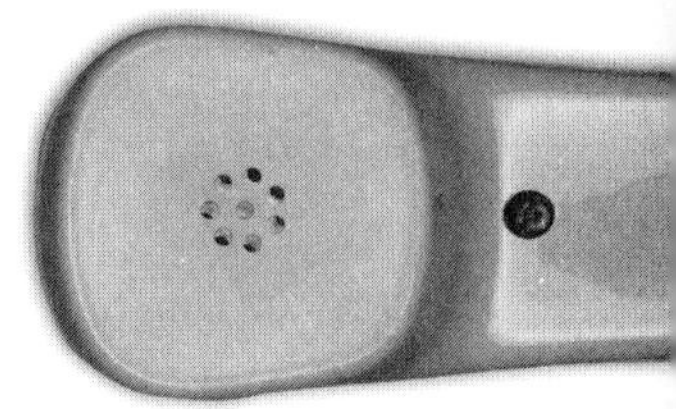

# Follow-up

TELEMARKETING EXPERTS DISAGREE ABOUT THE value of follow-up. Some argue that calling a prospect list twice is likely to generate only a marginal return over the first series of calls, and that sending e-mails to those who don't answer is of minimal value. These are the same people who think leaving voice-mail messages is a waste of time, since few calls are returned.

If you have an infinite number of telemarketers calling an infinite number of prospects, and the value of each prospect is exactly the same, then I agree with this assessment. If your chances of winning are only 50/50 no matter what coin you flip, you might as well flip a new one every time.

In reality, telemarketing is most cost efficient when a small, highly trained group of callers goes after a highly targeted audience. In this world, every prospect represents a significant potential sale and deserves personalized attention.

Ultimately, the issue is not how many potential buyers exist in the marketplace, but how many you can chase with the resources you have in a reasonable period of time. If you only have an hour a day, pick the best twenty-five. If you have eight hours a day, pick the best 200. Work these completely with repeated calls and other follow-up strategies until you're convinced that these prospects are either not interested or not reachable. Then move on to the next group.

## ACTION ITEMS

### Respond first to the interested.

If someone orders, communicate that order to the fulfillment part of your organization immediately upon receipt, or at least by the end of the day. For information requests, fill them (or have them filled) before you move to the next call. For lead generation, refer the lead to the appropriate sales rep by telephone and/or e-mail without delay.

## HAND-OFFS

### Transition leads immediately.

If your job is to generate qualified leads for outside sales reps, transition these leads as soon as you identify them.

The point at which a telemarketer should "hand off" a lead to an outside sales rep is a matter of interpretation among the parties. Generally, any prospect who is seriously interested in purchasing (e.g., asks for a demonstration or a face-to-face meeting, praises the product, mentions that a budget exists for the product, mentions that someone he or she knows has already purchased the product and likes it, mentions that the company is issuing a request-for-proposal to buy this kind of product soon, etc.) should be referred to the rep.

When you transition a qualified lead, take three steps:

*Prospect notification*—At the conclusion of your call, tell the decision maker that (the rep's name) will be contacting him soon to continue the discussion. Reiterate this information in a follow-up e-mail.

*Rep notification*—E-mail the rep responsible for the account, explaining the circumstances of the call and notifying him or her that you are, at that moment, transitioning the lead from telemarketing to outside sales. Make a follow-up phone call if necessary to discuss any details.

*Record keeping*—Indicate in your electronic database that the hand-off has taken place. Delete your name as the person responsible for the account and replace it with the name of the rep.

## REPEAT CALLS

### Keep trying.

If you can't reach a decision maker on the first call, and choose to make repeat calls, adopt a call schedule based on the number of prospects you're trying to reach and the relative value of each prospect. For high priority prospects, I suggest the following call sequence:

| | |
|---|---|
| Day 1 | 1st call; leave message |
| Day 3 | 2nd call; no message |
| Day 5 | 3rd call; no message |
| Day 7 | 4th call; leave message |
| Day 14 | 5th call; leave message |
| Day 21 | 6th call; leave message |
| Day 28 | 7th call; leave message |
| Month 2, 3, 4, 5, 6 | 8th/9th/10th call; leave message |
| Month 9, 12 | 11th/12th call; leave message |

## E-MAIL

### Couple with calls.

Whenever possible get the e-mail address of each prospect. Then send a brief follow-up note immediately after your call. Attach a collateral piece about your product (PDF format) with your letter. Create templates in your CRM software to automate the process. A sample e-mail might be:

*Wayne,*

*I tried to reach you today to introduce our new product called XYZ that will enable your company to . . .*

*Critical features include . . .*

*Our customers include . . .*

*For additional details, please visit our website at (company URL) and review the attached product description.*

*Please call me to arrange an online product demonstration at your convenience.*

*Best regards,*

## RECORD KEEPING

### Keep track of everything you do.

Immediately after hanging up, record the basic details of the call in the master database. If you spoke with the decision maker, what did the person say? Is there any interest? Were any objections stated? What follow-up was requested? The longer you wait to record the details of the call, the less you will remember. When you take follow-up action as a result of the call, record this in the contact record.

For common notes, you might want to abbreviate:

| | |
|---|---|
| NI | not interested |
| SI | sent information |
| LM | left message with an individual |
| LM/VM | left message on voice mail |
| BZ | line is busy |
| NA | no answer |
| OB | out-of-business/phone disconnected |

# PART 11

## SELF-MANAGEMENT

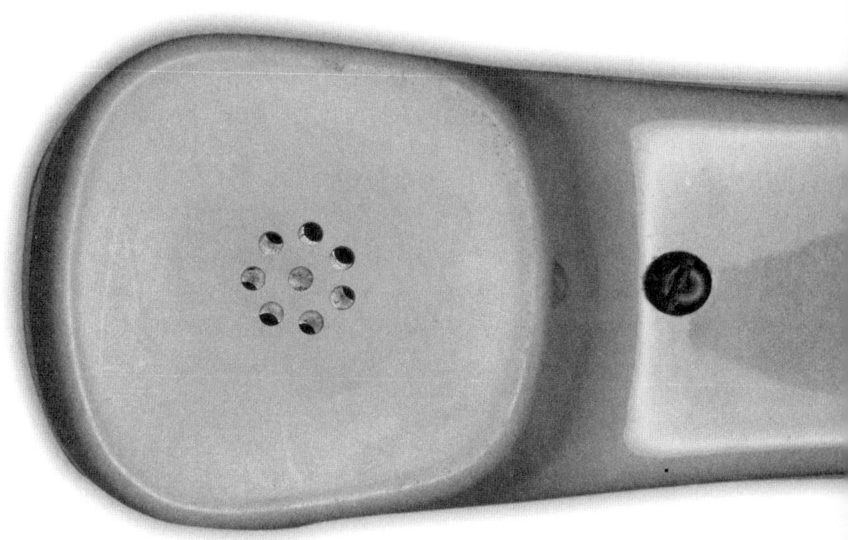

# CHAPTER FORTY

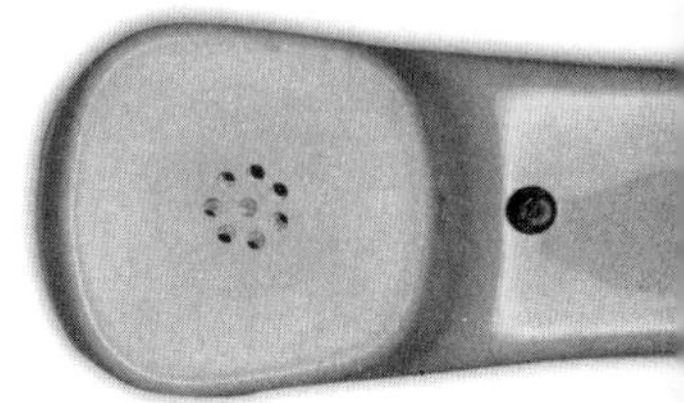

## Fear

NOTHING SCARES A SALES REP like cold calling! Time after time, the kick-ass superstar who can sell anything in a face-to-face meeting turns into Jell-O when he has to call a stranger on the phone.

Over the years, I've seen managers try all kinds of techniques to coerce their sales reps into calling new prospects. Typically, they start with earnest "encouragement," then shift to quotas, and end with gimmicks like "cold call Fridays" where everybody gathers in one place for a few hours once a month to commiserate, drink coffee, and make a handful of calls.

Regardless of the approach, most reps manage to escape without dialing the first number. Some beg off by saying that they're too busy with existing customers to chase new ones. Some are conveniently "in the field" when they're supposed to be on the phone. Some simply dismiss telemarketing as a waste of time.

I shouldn't complain. After all, if it weren't for "cold call anxiety syndrome," I might be flipping burgers today. All I have to say is "Yes, I do cold calls," and managers immediately usher me to a nearest phone. (Unfortunately, it's usually located in a windowless cubbyhole somewhere . . . but that's another story.)

So what's the problem? Why do grown men and women who are confident, self-motivated, and always ready to leap tall buildings in a single bound suddenly run when it's time to prospect for new customers over the phone?

The short answer is fear—illogical, uncontrollable fear. I should know. I'm always afraid when I start a series of calls, despite my many years of experience. When the time comes to dial that first number of the day, my heart beats faster, my hands get sweaty, and my teeth just naturally clinch. It happens every time.

## KISS OF DEATH

### Don't scare them away.

Sounding afraid is the last thing you want to do on the phone. The person you're calling is already nervous. He doesn't know whether to trust you or not. When you sound nervous, he subconsciously decides that his fears are justified. Rather than seeing you as a human being with normal insecurities, he thinks you have something to hide.

Is this fair? No. Is it real? Absolutely! Like the debtor who can't get a loan because he has debts, you can't win if you're desperate to win . . . or at least if you sound desperate. So even if you muster enough courage to dial the number, your fear of cold calling can poison the results.

## THE BOOGEYMAN

### Look under the bed.

So what do we fear about cold calling? The phone itself looks harmless enough, and I've never known an irate prospect who could reach through the line and grab me by the throat. You would think that reps would be much more afraid of face-to-face meetings, where they might have to run for the door after a bad appointment. On the phone, the worst case ends in a hang-up. No harm. No foul.

This contradiction tells us that fear of cold calling has nothing to do with real threats, and everything to do with the cobwebs in your own mind. While anxiety may seem irrational, it's still real to the person experiencing it. Unfortunately, ignoring your fears or dismissing them without examination doesn't make them disappear.

After ducking, hiding, and doing anything possible to ignore my fears for years, I finally learned that the only way to overcome a fear is to look it in the face. In the case of cold calling anxiety, I've learned that this monster has many faces.

*Fear of getting caught*—If you're using telemarketing to cheat, lie, or steal, you should be afraid. The threat is real. Eventually, the consequences of your actions will grab you from behind, or you'll drive yourself crazy looking over your shoulder. Either way, it's not a pretty picture. If you're a rip-off artist, stop reading this book; and repay your victims.

Ironically, the rest of us, who make an honest living selling reliable products at fair prices, often feel guilty too, even though we're not perpetrating any type of fraud. Maybe we feel uncomfortable violating the private space of those we call. Maybe we feel badly about using our persuasive powers to obtain money from strangers, even when the transaction is voluntary. Maybe we worry that the product we're selling will break down unexpectedly for some customer somewhere, even though our company guarantees to repair or replace it.

If you're an honest person and you still feel guilty about selling over the phone, ask yourself a few hard questions. Do you think it's morally wrong for a stranger to interrupt a decision maker in his office with an unsolicited phone call? If so, don't do it. Do you think it's morally wrong to sell something that the buyer had no intention of buying until you called him? If so, don't do it. Do you think it's morally wrong to sell something that might break down unexpectedly or out of warranty? If so, don't do it. If you can't escape a vague sense of guilt every time you dial a stranger's phone number, stop dialing.

On the other hand, if you believe that you're doing something to help your customers, you can feel strong and proud, call after call. You can handle the disdain and contempt that some calls may engender, because you know that you've doing the right thing.

Ultimately, your ability to sell depends upon your moral compass. With an unshakable conviction that your message is true and your intentions are good, you can overcome your fears and overcome the fears of those you call. As honest Abe said, you can't fool all the people all of the time. In the end, your customers will sense the truth about you. Believe in what you do, and others will believe too.

*Fear of failure*—Would you visit a doctor if you knew that 95 percent of his patients die within three months of seeing him? Probably not, unless the physician is the world's best oncologist and you have terminal cancer. Then that 5 percent success rate might not look so bad.

The same can be said for cold calling. On the surface, having ninety-five out of one hundred people saying "No" may not sound very successful. But if one of the five who say "Yes" translates into a million-dollar purchase, then the effort is certainly worthwhile.

In reality, the rep who's afraid to dial a stranger isn't thinking about dollars and cents. No, he's imagining the sick, sad feeling in his gut that comes from being personally rejected time after time. It's easy to say, "Don't take it personally," but it is personal. You're the one who's swinging. You're the one who's striking out. Who wants to be subjected to that kind of disappointment?

I'm no Sigmund Freud, but I think it's safe to say that our dread of humiliation starts early in life. Like Adam and Eve who discovered their nakedness one day, there is a moment when someone laughed at us and we suddenly felt self-conscious. As I remember it, someone making fun of you hurt more than being hit with a stick. A bruise on your arm would go away eventually, but a bruise on your ego seemed to last forever.

We are all social creatures, like it or not. We all want to be accepted. We all want to be part of the circle. We all want to hear applause, not boos.

Imagine that 100 people are in a long line in front of you. The first one walks up, puts his lips near your ear, and says with an irritated voice, "No!" The second one follows immediately behind the first and repeats, this time with a hint of anger, "No!" followed by the third, and fourth, on and on, each with his own version of the same two letter word, until the collective rejection of ninety-five people rings in your ears.

In the beginning of this process, you're not really affected by the people or their words. After all, they're just strangers. Their opinions mean nothing. After twenty or thirty repetitions, the whole thing seems boring, like a radio station with lousy music. At fifty, you're starting to get irritated by the drip, drip, drip of the same word over and over again. By seventy-five, you've had enough and just want to run. By the time all ninety-five of the nay-sayers have stabbed you in the ear, you realize that another emotion has replaced your anger. It's sadness, an irrational gripping depression that has fallen upon you like a fog and refuses to dislodge.

And then, when you don't think you can stand this kind of rejection for another second, number ninety-six walks up and says, "Yes!" You can't believe what you're hearing. Then ninety-seven, ninety-eight, ninety-nine, and one hundred repeat that incredible word again and again and again and again. "Yes! Hallelujah! Yes!" Was a sweeter sound every uttered?

Ultimately, your ability to survive and thrive in this roller-coaster environment is determined by the amount of approval you need. If you're the kind of person who craves constant affirmation, telemarketing will be impossible to bear. If you don't care about what other people think you'll survive the process, but you won't make the sales. Without an appreciation of the customer's problems and emotions, you'll be unable to establish the necessary trust upon which long-term selling relationships are based.

The trick is to care about the reactions of others, but not too much. Finding this balance takes time and a bit of inner soul searching. As with any other difficult situation, the fear of failure can be seen as either a problem or an opportunity. To move ahead in your work and in your life, use the constant rejection inherent in cold calling as a way of facing rejection in general. Confronting this monster, day after day, will make you a stronger, more confident person.

*Performance anxiety*—They say that most people consider public speaking to be one of their greatest fears. The heart of this phobia lies not in failing to influence the audience, but in merely making a credible, intelligent sounding presentation. Who wants to be the juggler that drops the ball or the actor who forgets his lines? Who wants to reach an important person on the phone and start stuttering?

The ability to perform under pressure is essential to telemarketing success. You have only a few seconds to create a favorable impression and to implant the basic message about your product in the distracted brain of a skeptical customer.

I'm reminded of a hard-nosed English teacher I had in high school, who subtracted ten points for every spelling error or punctuation error in our papers. I can remember spending twenty hours writing a dissertation comparing one work of literature to another, only to have my grade reduced from a "B" to a "D" due to the incorrect placement of two commas. After the first few weeks, you either dropped out of her class or learned to spell and punctuate correctly. I chose the latter.

Telemarketing is much the same. Often you're judged more for your mistakes than for the content of your message. Every time you tangle your words, stutter, say "uh," talk too loud or too soft, talk too fast or too slow, or fail to answer basic questions about your product, the listener sees a red flag. He may forgive you for one, maybe two minor errors (unlike my teacher), but don't count on it. In fact, the person you're calling is much more motivated to end the call than continue it. Every error gives him an excuse to hang up.

Considering all the pressure to deliver a flawless presentation every time, it's no wonder that anyone making cold calls gets nervous. For some this fear is too much to bear. For some, the sensation is not fear at all, but excited anticipation. My son was an excellent basketball player in high school. I watched every game. Frequently, the outcome of his games would be determined in the last minute of play by one shot, usually taken by my son. I asked him about the pressure, saying that I would have been too nervous to take the deciding shot. His answer was short and unequivocal: "Dad, I want the ball!" For some, high pressure situations are unconquerable torture, for others they are exhilarating adventure.

Fortunately, performance anxiety can be cured more easily than many other phobias. If you're afraid of flubbing the words, create a simple, easy flowing script and practice it over and over until the words fall effortlessly from your lips. If you're afraid of sounding ignorant about the product's basic features and benefits, study them until you understand them, then post them nearby when you call. If you're paranoid about a particular kind of person you might encounter, such as a bully or know-it-all, imagine talking with that person again and again until you feel comfortable.

Both the challenge and the beauty of cold calling is that it's over in a matter of seconds. Like an actor performing a movie take, all you have to do is deliver a few lines well.

> "The single most important thing you can do for sweaty palms is rehearse. The second most important thing you can do for sweaty palms is rehearse. Guess what the third thing is?"
>
> —David Peoples

*Jerk phobia*—My deepest fear in cold calling is not how well I'll deliver my script or how many people will be interested in my pitch, but whether I'll encounter a serious jerk on the other end of the line. While this rarely happens, I'm always affected when it does.

Recently, after researching the Net, I found the name and phone number of a decision maker who was particularly difficult to identify. Enthusiastic about my important message, I called him:

Bright and cheery, I said "Hello! How are you today?"

"Who is this?" the invisible ogre on the line barked back.

"This is Stewart Rogers with ABC calling about XYZ," I sputtered.

"How did you get this number?" he demanded to know.

After I explained my source, he shouted, "This is a private number. I don't know how you got it. Never call here again!"

Boom! The phone slammed in my ear.

Gee, that was fun, kind of like a piano landing on my head out of a clear blue sky.

Of course, the real villain never actually touched me. His punch was only a sound in my ear. Why should I care?

This kind of call continues to affect me, because I care about everyone I call. I dial each number with an open heart and a sincere desire to meet the needs of the person I'm calling. In this sense, I'm vulnerable. I am touched by the words I hear and the emotions I sense beneath the words. This is my strength as a telemarketer and my Achilles heel.

So, how often does a rude, obnoxious psycho jerk answer the phone? In my experience as a business-to-business telemarketer, these kinds of calls are few and far between. I probably reach a needlessly irate businessperson less than one time in 1,000.

What can you do to prevent this from happening? Nothing. It's an unfortunate part of the territory.

If it happens to you, cuss the jerk out (mentally), then take yourself to lunch. You've been wronged. You deserve better.